WE DO NOT DIE ALONE:

"JESUS IS COMING TO GET ME IN A WHITE PICKUP TRUCK"

Marilyn A. Mendoza, PhD.

Foreword by
Sylvia Rayfield & Loretta Manning

ICAN PUBLISHING INC.
162 Lumpkin County Parkway, Suite 9
Dahlonega, Georgia 30533
1.866.428.5589
www.icanpublishing.com

Cover Design by Teresa Davidson, Greensboro, North Carolina.
Proofed by Patricia Kleinhans, Dahlonega, GA

ICAN PUBLISHING INC.
162 Lumpkin County Parkway, Suite 9
Dahlonega, Georgia 30533

ISBN# 978-0-976 1029-5-3

Library of Congress Publication Data 2008932975

Mendoza, Marilyn A.
*We Do Not Die Alone: "Jesus Is Coming to Get Me in a White Pickup
Truck"*
First Edition September 2008

TABLE OF CONTENTS

"This world is not conclusion:
A sequel stands beyond"
—Emily Dickinson, Poet

This book is dedicated to my parents,
Ann and Jacob Allen
who are waiting to take me home.

Acknowledgements

Bette Davis is credited with having said that old age is not for sissies. I would change that to say that writing a book and getting it published is not for sissies. Even knowing the perils involved, it is still a difficult process. I was fortunate to have many supporters along the way. Those who helped opened doors for me were: Trish Clark, RN, DON at Our Lady of Wisdom Nursing Home in New Orleans; Opal Carriere, RN, Administrator of Serenity Hospice Services of New Orleans; Jamey Boudreaux, MSW, M.Div., Executive Director of the Louisiana and Mississippi Hospice and Palliative Care Organization and Sandy H. Bryan, MHA, BSN, RN, BC Clinical Research Specialist, Shore Health System of Maryland. I would like to extend special recognition to Alex Weiss, RN whose assistance in the initial stages of this project was so helpful.

I have been fortunate to share my life with Martha Pollock and Christine Costello, PhD, my best friends. I cannot imagine how empty life would have been without them. They have always been a guiding presence for me and especially during the writing of this book. They read many drafts of the manuscript, made suggestions, and corrected my grammar and punctuation. They were my best cheerleaders. There are not words to thank them for all they have done for me.

Peggy Brown, LCSW, BCD, a writer herself, was not only supportive but introduced me to Sylvia Rayfield, my publisher. For that, I will always be grateful. My business manager, Connie Varuso, had to listen to my trials and tribulations on an almost daily basis. She deserves a medal as well as my thanks. Martha McQuitty, R.N. and Lauren Miller offered continued encouragement throughout this process. Thank you.

Sylvia Rayfield and Loretta Manning at ICAN Publishing, Inc., were able to see the potential of my manuscript when others could not. I will forever be grateful to them for their kindness and guidance during the completion of this book.

My husband, John, deserves special credit. He was a

lifesaver. Having just published a book, he was the perfect person to provide moral and professional support. Who better to empathize with you than someone who has been through it himself. He encouraged me and believed in me. Jessica and Matthew, my children, each supported me in their own way.

Matthew was my computer consultant. Whenever something would go wrong, I would call on him. This was a great lesson for him in developing a tolerance for frustration. Jessica, a photographer, took my picture for the cover.

Finally, my gratitude goes to all the nurses and dying patients whose information is contained in this book. They will never know how many lives have been touched as a result of their participation.

FOREWORD

Like an escort thru profound events, Marilyn Mendoza reports the vast experiences of nurses and their encounters with soul. *We Do Not Die Alone: "Jesus Is Coming to Get Me in a White Pickup Truck"* is an amazing chronicle of the nurses who have been present at the bedside of their dying patients. Many dying patients have the ability to see an essence from the spirit world that calms their fears and provides their attending families with a feeling of peace and closure. Numerous nurses have observed the experiences of their patients seeing the spirits who come to help their patients make an easier transition.

Witnessing this has made a deep impact on the nurses themselves. Sometimes our zeal in trying to "keep them alive" causes us to lose sight of the other happenings at the time of death. This book gives us the confidence to be curious about who is visiting our patient. The author brings alive for nurses and those of us who encounter dying people the message that one of our highest callings is to empower the dying with worth and dignity.

The title *We Do Not Die Alone: "Jesus Is Coming to Get Me in a White Pickup Truck"* is notice for all of us to be cognizant of the spiritual transition. Nurses are not the only professionals that will be impacted by this publication. Hospice workers, psychologists, psychiatrists, social workers and anyone caring for a dying family member, friend or interested in their own "soul work" will find this work as we did, inspirational.

Dr. Mendoza also reports other consequential encounters with spirits after death. Often these encounters provide the living with an overpowering sense of a guide for their future life. She provides strategies for nursing students and nursing faculty to reflect on these experiences of others in order to develop their own professional and personal understanding and awareness while providing both the spiritual and physical care for the dying patient.

Health care workers, patients, and families in general do not tend to talk about these encounters with the soul. Some are concerned that others will "think they are nuts." This book facilitates conversations to discuss our experiences and thus deepen our own soul connections, resulting in a peaceful dying process for us all.

Sylvia Rayfield
Loretta Manning
ICAN Publishing, Inc.

PREFACE

As a young child, I was very close to my mother. When I was 13 years old, my father died suddenly. His death only made my attachment to my mother stronger. I felt she was all I had and I was so afraid of losing her. I developed a painful separation anxiety disorder that lasted into my college years. I would dissolve into a puddle of tears whenever I thought of her not being with me. During this time of my life, I was extremely compliant. Anything Mother wanted me to do, I did. It was important to me to please her. As I got older and became more independent, problems began. I realized that my mom liked to be in control and so did I.

We had our struggles like all mothers and daughters. No one could make me as angry as Mother or make me feel as loved. Our battles were not unique. But even through the most difficult of times, I knew that I could count on her and that she would always be there for me. When my family and I decided to move from Chicago to New Orleans, it was always understood that Mother would come live with us. So at the age of 80, Mother sold our family home in Georgia and came to New Orleans. The move revitalized her. She was still very active. She managed the house, helped with the children and cooked. Her assistance was invaluable, as I was trying to establish a professional reputation in a new community. As time moved on, Mother became more limited in what she could do. This was a difficult adjustment for her, having been so active all her life. She became very unhappy and irritable. Mom began to have more physical problems including a stroke, fractured hip and the loss of her vision. With each incident it was harder for her to come back, but Mother was not one to give up. There does, however, come a time when age overcomes us all. Mom became one of the very old. After her 95th birthday, it was noticeable that she was starting to decline. One morning, I found Mom on the floor next to her bed. She had gotten up at night and collapsed on the floor with a broken leg. At the hospital, Mother began to decline rapidly. The doctors called us in on several occasions as the end seemed imminent. When hope was gone, we brought her home to die.

We had round-the-clock sitters and hospice involved in her care. It seemed as though there was always someone in the house. One Sunday when Mother and I were alone, she called out to me. She wanted to tell me that she was ready to go. I went over to her bed, held her, kissed her and told her it was O.K. if she wanted to go. She closed her eyes. It got very still and I braced myself for what was to come, the moment I had dreaded my entire life. Suddenly, Mother opened her eyes and in an angry voice said, "They won't let me go! They say it's not my number." I had to laugh. I did not know you had to have a number to die. I was also relieved that my mother was still alive.

Mom died on Sunday, June 4th, 2000. She was just three weeks away from her 96th birthday. I had wanted to be with her to hold her hand as she passed on to another life just as she had been with me in this life. But Mom had other plans. After her death, I realized what my mother's number was. Forty years earlier, my father died on Sunday, June 4th. It was not until several months after my Mother's death that I came across information that her father had also died on June 4th. Since then, every June 4th my brother and I call to check on each other.

In life, Mother helped to shape who I am. In death, she gave new direction and purpose to my life. After my experiences with Mother, I was more certain than ever that I wanted to work with the dying and their families. I feel the work I am currently doing with the bereaved and this book are a testament to my experiences with her. I have been to many bereavement workshops and conferences. It seems that many of us who enter this field have been spurred on by someone's death; it is frequently our moms.

My original idea for this book was to present research investigating the impact of death related experiences on nurses. Being a PhD, research was what I knew. But from the comments of others, I came to realize that much was being missed by only reporting the facts. This is an area where our hearts and souls should be involved. Data cannot give us hope for the future but reading these reports can.

This book is a description of experiences reported by nurses caring for the dying. It is meant to facilitate and improve care of the dying especially by new nurses or any individual that is present at the time of death. The more I worked with this book, the more obvious it became, that this information is important for all interested in learning more about our transition from this life. It is my fervent hope that the awe and wonder of these phenomena will bring peace to those who read this as we all eventually face our own time of passing.

Chapter 1: Introduction

"The longest journey is the journey inward."
Dag Hammarskjold

A male hospice patient in his 60's with cancer was minimally responsive and nearing transition when he sat up and began to call for his mother. He was smiling joyfully and described his mother as coming to get him in a white pickup truck. She was sitting in the passenger seat next to Jesus who was driving the truck. His little pet bird was sitting on Jesus' shoulder. The man died shortly after this. On his wife's return home, she found the little pet bird was dead in its cage.

An elderly female who was declining rapidly kept saying, "Ike, Ike (Ike was her brother), there's Ike, he has come to get me."

A 98 year old female told me the night before she died that it would be her last night on earth. She spoke with many of her dead relatives. She said they were waiting for her.

A 10 year old boy said, "Angels are lifting me up to the light. They are so pretty, Mommy." Then the boy died.

When my own mother died, I was comforted by mom's report that her own mother had "come to get her."

These are just some of the stories that were collected while conducting a survey on the effects of deathbed visions on nurses. A deathbed vision (DBV) is a vision or experience that the individual has before dying. It may occur immediately before death or days or even weeks prior. Patients have reported visions of dead family members, religious figures or beautiful scenery. With a DBV, unlike a Near Death Experience (NDE), death is final and no one comes back to talk about the experience. Other terms used for Deathbed Visions have been Nearing Death Awareness,[1] Death Related Visions,[2] Deathbed Apparitions,[3] and Death-Related Sensory Experiences.[4] For the purposes of this book, these experiences will be referred to as deathbed visions (DBVs).

Deathbed visions do not always take place in bed, however, as in the account of Sam Kinison's death. Sam Kinison was an entertainer in the late 1980's and early 1990's. He and his new wife were driving to Nevada and were hit by a pickup truck. Sam was not wearing a seatbelt and hit the windshield. Onlookers including his wife said he looked normal and they thought he would pull through. He began speaking to something unseen and said "I don't want to die." It then appeared that he was having a conversation with someone and said…"But why?" "Okay, Okay, Okay.". Witnesses said his last okay was said softly and comfortably as if he were talking to someone he loved. He was taken to the hospital and was dead on arrival.[5]

HOW THE EXPERIENCES WERE COLLECTED

The accounts were a product of a survey conducted among various nursing professionals in Louisiana prior to Hurricane Katrina in 2005 and in Maryland in 2006. There were 234 respondents (221 Registered Nurses and 13 Licensed Practical Nurses) from hospices, hospitals, nursing conferences, nursing homes and home health facilities. The forms were filled out anonymously and with the exception of age and sex, no identifying information was given about the patients. The survey consists of 14 items which were developed to examine nurses' perceptions of deathbed visions. The last item was a blank page in which nurses were asked to write about some of their more memorable experiences. The stories in this book are the result of these responses. The nurses' words are as they were written and are found in italics throughout the book.

Chapters 1 through 10 contain the accounts. Chapter 11 discusses after-death communications. Chapter 12 is devoted to exploring the history, theory and controversy surrounding DBVs. Chapter 13 examines nursing, individuals and spirituality. Chapter 14 is about caring for the caretaker, while instructions for the caretaker are found in Chapter 15. Chapter 16 contains concluding thoughts. As you read this book on deathbed visions, you may wonder why Near Death Experiences are referenced so often. Given the lack of research on DBVs, the findings from NDEs are used here as a springboard for understanding the DBV. I also have taken the liberty of including several personal stories related to my own parents' deaths as well as stories from my private practice about after-death communication.

When reading the accounts that follow, it is natural to wonder about the meaning of these experiences. No one really wants to contemplate his or her own death but we are often more willing to explore this area in the abstract. What happens to us when we die has been something that has intrigued man back to the time of the Neanderthals. Their ritual burial behavior of the dead suggests that there was concern about what happened after this life. The afterlife has been depicted in art and literature throughout time and in many cultures. The depictions are often similar as exemplified by medieval European and Asian art.[6] Even with all the research in the past 30 years, there is still no universally agreed upon position as to what happens when we die. The fact that these deathbed phenomena occur is well documented. It is their meaning that is still in question. This book does not proclaim to answer what is the most profound and universal question for mankind. Rather, the hope is that the stories will stimulate the reader's curiosity about the dying process and bring attention to the importance of the nurse's role in end of life care.

As you read the experiences, try thinking about yourself in the role of the dying or the family member and imagine what it would be like for you. What thoughts and feelings might you have if this were happening to you? In Rachel Stanworth's article[7] on the role of being attentive as a way of providing spiritual care for the dying, she quotes the words of the French philosopher, Jean Francois. A few days before his death he said "What do I care about deep existential issues now. I just want someone to hold my hand."

Chapter 2: Accounts of Dead Relatives

"Do not stand at my grave and weep.
I am not there, I do not sleep."
Kelly L. Delaney

Who better to hold our hands when dying than a family member? It appears from the following accounts that comfort is achieved whether the family member is alive or not. The majority (57%) of the deathbed experiences from the survey had to do with deceased relatives. Many reflected long awaited family reunions and the calming and peaceful effect deathbed visions had on the patients and those around them.

> *An older woman dying of cancer told me about her sister and how the woman had come to see her in her hospital room. Then the patient started telling me in a very calm matter of fact way that her sister had been dead for over forty years. The patient had always been very fussy and short with the staff during her stay but after the appearance of her dead sister she became very calm and seemed happy.*

> *A hundred year old female described seeing her deceased relatives, yet knew that no one else could see them but her. She appeared to be in two worlds at the same time. It was very moving spiritually and emotionally.*

> *A 73 year old female, about three to four weeks before she died, was angry and yelling at her*

deceased relatives. She was shouting out and calling them by name which was rather hard for me since I did not see anyone else in the room with her. Soon after this episode she became very calm and suddenly seemed at peace with her impending death. She never called out or spoke again after that. She died the next day.

Many times it is the mother who comes to retrieve her child, no matter how "old" that child may be. Mothers are frequently appearing figures in the deathbed visions throughout this book. Perhaps it is true when they say that a mother's work is never done. Nurses know that when the dying begin calling for their mothers that death is not far behind.

An 80 year old female was dying at home with hospice when she started speaking to her dead mother. She said her mother was in the bedroom with us. The patient appeared to be very comforted to see her mother.

A patient dying of cancer had been very restless throughout the night. In the early morning she appeared to calm down and rest. She opened her eyes and stared fixedly into the corner of the room where no one was standing. She said, "Mom, I'm so glad to see you." And she smiled. After saying this, the tension in the room from the family eased. After the patient's comment, she died peacefully.

An elderly woman kept talking to her mother and her brother. Both of whom had been deceased. She carried on several conversations with them. She would smile and drift off to sleep. Finally she talked to her deceased relatives and agreed with them that it was time to go home. She died.

My father saw my mother in the kitchen and had a warm loving conversation with her. My mother had been dead for seven years. Later, my father told us he would be going on a trip with mom on Wednesday. He died on Friday. "Mom always ran late." So we knew it was her. My father had been very comforted by having seen mom, as was the rest of the family.

A patient was in severe respiratory distress and was having extreme difficulty breathing. After he told me he had seen his dead mother standing by his bed, he suddenly completely relaxed, smiled and then died.

One patient of mine spent several days struggling with the dying process as if she were fighting it or waiting for someone. Her son-in-law came in and told her he was her son and that it was okay for her to leave and go meet the rest of her family. She immediately became quiet, called out to her mother as if she saw her and passed on.

A common theme underlies these encounters. When the dying see a deceased relative, it brings them peace and comfort.

A hospice patient who had been struggling with severe pain was in the last minutes of life when he suddenly looked toward the wall, smiled, relaxed his body and closed his eyes. He then called out his dead sister's name and seconds later died.

While working on a Med/Surg Unit, I was giving nursing care to a female dying of cancer. She was about 68 years old and had a large family.

Someone from the family visited everyday. The patient was hallucinating off and on because of pain medication given for dressing changes. When the medication took effect she always spoke about Shirley. She spoke to Shirley as though she was in the room. She seemed to feel safe and taken care of when she knew Shirley was sitting at her bedside. I asked a family member, "Who was Shirley?"(thinking she was a living member of the family). I was told that Shirley was her dead sister who had died at a young age (22). They were close and grew up together and took care of each other. The patient seemed comforted and safe with her sister. The experience made me feel Shirley was my patient's angel at her deathbed, there to bring her comfort.

I was present at the time of the passing of an elderly female who was within 30 minutes of dying. She had been sleeping for eight hours and was reported as having been unresponsive during that time. She opened her eyes and pointed to the upper corner of the room. She began to have what appeared to be a very pleasant conversation. She was smiling, nodding and speaking. I asked who she was talking to and she said "it's my husband who I haven't seen in years." She continued with her conversation for about three minutes, smiled, closed her eyes and said "I am ready to go now." She passed away 30 minutes later.

I have had several disoriented, angry and combative patients who started talking to dead family members. The patients always seemed to calm down, smile and begin to appear very happy once they have been visited by their family.

Watching people die in pain and agony is highly distressing and is often the source of burnout for nurses who are part of this process. Deathbed visions can help provide relief not only for the patient but also for the caregiver as the following descriptions suggest.

> *A 52 year old female was dying of a failed transplant. She was terrified of dying and often spoke about how she was never going to give into death. Two days before her demise, she kept looking over my shoulder and laughing and smiling at someone standing behind me. There was no one there. I asked the patient who she was talking to and she told me her dead father. Then she stated "Okay, all right. It's O.K., I'm not afraid." And then she died very peacefully, smiling. It was such a relief to finally see the poor woman at peace.*

> *An elderly female was smiling and reaching out for her sister (who had died many years before). The patient tried to get out of the bed to go to be closer to the vision of her sister. The patient talked with the vision and was happy and smiling as if her sister was right there in the room with her. Even though she was very debilitated and nonambulatory, she kept trying to get up and kept reaching her arms out for her sister as if to touch or hug her. I felt very blessed and very close to the Lord at this time. Her family members were there in the hospital room and also felt close to the Lord. I especially like Hospice work because I feel blessed to be with people as they die. It is very spiritual."*

Often, more than one deceased relative comes to help the patient transition. Even though the patient may not recognize relatives by sight, there is a sense of knowing and being connected to them.

> *A 40 year old female at the time of her death said she had spoken to many of her deceased relatives. She knew some of them and the others she did not know. When she finally did let go of her life, she died with the most peaceful expression on her face.*

> *A 63 year old female several days before she died was talking to her deceased father and other dead relatives she had never met before. It had a very calming effect on her.*

In some instances, these visions of the dead create great excitement for the patient as they look forward to reuniting with their deceased relatives. Imagine that, instead of being fearful, one can actually be excited to leave this life.

> *Several patients stated they saw dead relatives, mostly their parents or a dead spouse. The vision seemed to relax them at first but then they would become agitated. It was like they were really anxious to see their family members again. They were all eager to talk to me about their visions but they were even more anxious to join their loved ones on the other side. It's funny to me because as a nurse I never thought I would take care of patients who were eager to die.*

As people go through their preparations for dying, they frequently look to resolve conflict and to give and ask for forgiveness. There is a need to complete unfinished business so that all involved can be at peace.

> *An 80 year old female told me she saw her dead daughter at her bedside one morning. She then began to tell me about her troubled relationship and how she and her daughter had fought before her daughter's death ten years before. She told me her daughter said she was not angry anymore and the elderly patient became so happy. She suddenly looked forward to her death. She said she was ready to go "home" and be with her family.*

> *A patient dying of AIDS talked to his dead parents who he had walked out on many years before. He said it was the first time he could remember he and his parents ever really talking. I remember he looked over at me, seemed so happy, and then he died.*

Many nurses reported that family members were comforted when their loved one spoke about seeing dead relatives. These experiences were reassuring and comforting for the family left behind as well as for those transitioning.

> *A woman dying of brain cancer opened her eyes and stared at her son and husband standing by her hospital bed. She said to them, " there's mom, see her?" The family members told the woman they could not see her mother. She then stated, "She's right there, see her?" She then closed her eyes and took one last breath. The experience was extremely peaceful and very comforting to the family.*

> *A patient saw her dead husband who she said had come to get her. She told her family with her*

in the room that she was happy to be joining her husband. She looked so peaceful after that and her family said they knew she wasn't going to be alone anymore.

It is not unusual for these deathbed experiences to be profoundly moving for the nurse, caregivers and family. The dyings' last words can be very reassuring for their loved ones.

I had a patient in the hospital that was semi-comatose and would awaken for only periods of two to three minutes a couple of times a day. His skin had started to cool and his eyes had become glassy. He also had a death rattle and 35 to 40 second periods of apnea (periods of breathlessness). I had been sitting with his wife giving her moral support. After about two hours he opened his eyes and looked over at us. He looked over to me and said, "Hello pretty lady." I said, "Hello, how are you?" He said, "I'm tired. My cousins are here, we're going home." His wife said, " Your cousins are here? But you are already home." He looked at her and said, "I love you and I'm ready to go home. I'll always be watching out for you and (their 6 month old daughter)." He died a half an hour later.

Sometimes family members who appear to the dying are accompanied by dead pets, like the pet bird in the initial story. Maybe it is true that "all dogs do go to heaven."

A 67 year old female saw her husband (who had died 4 years earlier) and her 22 year old dog that was also dead in a vision. She stated her husband had taken her hand and along with the old dog he told her he would show her the path to follow to be able to die peacefully.

A 30 year old female dying of brain cancer spoke of seeing her favorite horse she had owned when she was a young girl. Her mother sitting at her bedside stated she wasn't surprised the old gray mare had come back for her daughter. 'They had been inseparable in life,' the mother stated.

The person we might expect to see is often not the one who comes to be with us. This is one of the arguments that Osis and Haradlsson, [1] authors of a cross cultural study on DBVs, used to support their hypothesis of the existence of an afterlife. If DBV's were merely wish fulfillment, then we would only see those whom we would expect such as close family members. Many are surprised by who does come at the end.

A 70 year old female saw a lady she did not know in a vision. She was not fearful but curious about the woman. The figure was always reported by the patient to be standing in the corner. I encouraged the patient to talk to the figure and over time the patient became comfortable with the vision being there. Before she died, a few days after the vision appeared, the patient told that the stranger had actually been a friend she had worked with many years before who had died in a car accident. She said her friend had told her that she had been sent to get her.

A 68 year old male one day asked me, "Who is that standing behind you with the white suit on?" I told the patient, "I don't see anyone but I know you do." The patient then stated, "I can't see his face because he is standing directly behind you." I finished performing my care and left the patient's room. The patient's wife was walking down the hallway and asked me, "How's he today?" I said, "He's about the same but he is seeing someone in the room with him dressed in a white suit." The wife turned very pale and said to me, "You are kidding right?" She paused and added, "His best friend died last year and we buried him in his favorite white suit." The patient died the very same day.

———◆◆◆———

The next two reports describe how the patients' visions also felt very real to the nurses. Many times these experiences are truly "hair raising."

The patient did not appear frightened but I was somewhat afraid because it seemed as if the person or persons were right in the room with us. It seemed so real to the patient, they really believed in what they saw. It gave me goose bumps.

Patients express the vision as like "a dream" that is real. Sometimes I felt I could reach out and touch the person's family member who was visiting. Sometimes patients can't explain what they saw but they say the name of the deceased person and appear to be having some sort of visual hallucination.

———◆◆◆———

"Tomorrow I shall no longer be here"
Nostradamus, prophet

It is not unusual for the dying to "know" the day and time when they will die. Many times, this knowledge is given to them through their visions. In general these times can be amazingly accurate.

> *A patient told me of his deceased mother and father who were coming to get him <u>even though the patient had no clinical indications that he was going to die</u>. He said his parents told him that his time was up and he was going home with them. He asked me to call his children for him and tell them to come to the hospital. At the end of my shift his children came and the patient then announced to his family that he was going to die. His children did not believe him. The next day I came back to the unit to work and learned the man had died during the night. I guess his parents had been right after all.*

> *My mother-in-law was talking to her deceased sister and husband. She kept looking at one spot up on the ceiling. She told my deceased father-in-law that she was tired and would be joining him. She told him today would be the day they would be together again. She died about an hour later.*

> *A 70 year old female nursing home patient asked me to call her family to come and visit because she would be dead before Christmas (4 days away). <u>No imminent medical crisis was apparent at the time</u> but the patient said she was told by dead relatives to "get ready". On the day of her death she began talking to those dead relatives. She died on Christmas day.*

Deceased family members often seem to work together to help the dying transition, as in the following story:

> *A dying female patient told me her dead husband*

*was visiting her. But he had told her he was not
there to take her "home". He told the patient that
her mother would be coming to get her when it
was her time. The patient died two days later on
Mothers' Day.*

———————◆———————

"Get my swan suit ready"
Anna Pavlova, ballerina

Death as a journey is a frequent theme among the dying.
There is often a sense of urgency about this as the patient does
not want to be late for his conveyance to the other world.
When patients begin to talk about moving or traveling, it is
another signal that death is imminent.

*An 82 year old male hours before his death was visited
by his two deceased brothers who came to take him
"on a train trip." They told him to get his pants on
and get ready for his trip. The patient then insisted
that I help him pick a pair of pants for his trip. I did
so and helped him put them on. He was peaceful after
that and slipped quietly away that same night.*

*Twice, I have had patients try to get out of bed, stating
that they had to catch a train or had to go somewhere.*

Sometimes the patient may be ready to die only to find
out it is not yet time. While this is almost always found
in the Near Death Experience, it is not as common in
deathbed visions.

*I will tell you about my first deathbed experience.
I arrived at my patient's home and was greeted by
her husband. He told me his wife was acting very
strange. When I entered the patient was sitting up
in the bed. She had COPD (chronic obstructive
pulmonary disease) and was very short of breath*

when she spoke. She was looking up at the corner of the room, at the ceiling. She was talking to her sister as if she were in the room. I questioned her husband about this and he said she had been dead for ten years. I sat next to the patient and listened. She did not seem to realize that we were in the room. She kept calling her sister's name and asking, "When are you coming to get me? Why do I have to wait? Please don't leave me here. I'm ready." I listened to the patient for about 30 minutes and decided to speak to her. I asked "Are you alright." She responded "Yes," and then went back to finish her conversation with her sister. The patient died two days later.

Sometimes the opposite can occur when patients want to delay death and are told they need to leave now.

My mother died of cancer at home under Hospice care. When she was near death, it was only my daughter and I with her. She had just talked to my sister by phone who had told her she would be leaving that morning to make the trip to see her. My mother who had not spoken in several weeks due to the weakening effects of the chemotherapy drugs suddenly said "I can't go now. I need to wait." I asked her several times who she was talking to but she never told me. I assumed she was waiting for my sister to come. She said several more times "No, not yet. I want to wait" Then my mother said "Oh, all right" and passed away.

An elderly patient of mine had been lying unresponsive in bed and suddenly she sat up, stretched up her arms and said "I'm not ready." Then she died.

One of the nurses in the survey best summed up the experience of having family members appear in the patients' deathbed vision when she said:

> *I've seen patients die with their dead relatives standing by and I have seen patients die with only their living relatives in the room. I prefer those deaths where you know someone has come to get them. Then you know there is something more than what you see in this realm, it adds to the mystery of life and death. At least for me, it keeps me hopeful that when it is my time to go, someone I love will come back to get me.*

Chapter 3: Jesus and Angels

"I see Heaven open and Jesus at the right hand of God"
Thomas Cranmer, the Archbishop of Canterbury

Many times it is not a family member who comes for us but a spiritual being. Religious icons and angels were the second most frequently appearing (13%) figures in the survey. Several of the dying saw Jesus, while the majority saw angels. Melvin Morse, M.D., a pediatrician and neuroscientist who studies Near Death Experiences in children, states that at least 50% of the children in his studies saw angels. Since there was no information as to the religious affiliation of the patients, a correlation of the vision and belief was not possible. In these stories, as well as in other accounts in the literature, involving religious figures, their visitations bring the same sense of comfort to the dying as seeing old friends and family again.

> *My own daughter passed away at age 33. She told the nurse and her family "Jesus is coming to get me" and passed on within the hour.*

> *My grandmother told me that when my grandfather was dying that he saw the Blessed Virgin Mary dressed in blue and smiling.*

> *My first cancer patient saw "The Blessed Mother". She had been in severe pain which stopped with her vision.*

> *My mother who had a seven year battle with renal cell carcinoma awakened one night to see Jesus standing in her bedroom doorway surrounded by a bright light. She was frightened and hid under the covers. When she peeked out later, he was*

gone. She told me the next day that she was ashamed that she had hidden from Him. She felt he was coming for her and she was not ready.

———◆———

In working with the dying, nurses are exposed to a variety of religious beliefs and attitudes, from the extremely religious to atheism. In the stories that follow, Jesus came independent of strength of belief.

A non religious 68 year old male kept looking to the ceiling and when I asked him what he was looking at he replied, "Jesus". I asked him what Jesus was saying to him and the patient said, "Nothing. He's just looking at me. What should I do?" I told the patient to talk to Jesus and tell him what's in your heart. Minutes later he said Jesus had left. I asked him if he had talked to Jesus and he said yes. The patient stated that he had asked Jesus to help him and Jesus had said he would be there when the man crossed over. The patient died two days later very comfortably.

A retired nun told me about having a conversation with Jesus and being lifted from the bed towards the gates of heaven. The area had shiny gates with patches of clouds. The feeling was light and lifted her towards the gates of heaven.

An 80 year old male who was not conscious kept hollering out for Jesus like he was attending a great church service. He died the next day.

A lady in her 80's who was dying held her arms out and was speaking to the Lord. "I'm ready Lord" and a minute later, she was dead.

———◆———

The remaining types of religious figures in these descriptions were angels and figures of light. Stories about angels being involved in our lives go back to biblical times when they were messengers, helpers and protectors. It would make sense then that they would appear at our dying. It is said that we all have a guardian angel. It appears that the younger the patients are, the more likely they are to see angels.[1]

> A 6 year old female, while being held by her mother and rocked during the dying process, comforted her mother by telling her, "Look mom, it's like you said. There are angels everywhere— Jesus sent the angels to get me." The mother questioned her daughter and again the child explained that her hospital room was filled with angels that Jesus had sent to get her. The child told her mother she was not frightened. The child died in her mother's arms soon after.

> A seven year old girl saw visions of her deceased grandfather several days before her death. He would stand at her door and motion for her to come with him. At the time of her death, she looked out the window and said to me "look at all those angels out there." I said "what do they want?" she said "they want me to come play with them." I said "go ahead." She died shortly after that. I am convinced that near death experiences are real and what is seen is as it is. I am convinced that there is life after death.

> The experience that stands out the most for me was with a 5 or 6 year old on the Pediatric unit. The child was about to have heart surgery. She talked with the staff and family about how she felt about it. She stated she was not worried because

God and her angels told her everything would be alright. She spoke more about what would be happening and how her grandparents (deceased) would be there to see her through it. She died in surgery. We all knew she was at peace.

Angels' visits, however, are not limited to children. They visit the elderly as well.

An elderly female who was alert and oriented spoke to me of how angels had gathered in around her hospital bed and were ready to take her home. She died peacefully a short time later.

A 77 year old female dying of a bad heart saw angels in the room with her moments before her heart stopped and she died.

A patient dying of AIDS saw angels on the ceiling. He died talking to them. This definitely comforted the patient and the family.

Sometimes the dying receive visits from both family members and religious figures.

A 90 year old female had been speaking to dead family members for hours. But then her manner changed and she started talking about the angels made of bright lights filling her room. Then she took a last breath, smiled and died.

Chapter 4: Beautiful Places

"It is very beautiful over there."
Dying words of Thomas Edison, inventor

Beautiful is a word often used to describe visions of spiritual beings. However, there are other types of deathbed visions that involve beauty. These are the beautiful places and gardens. Patients describe significant perceptual enhancement with these visions. They describe the gardens as beautiful beyond anything seen on earth. Colors are vibrant and intense. The dying often say that there are no colors on earth that are even comparable. The gardens look perfect as one might expect the Garden of Eden to have been. These visions made up 12% of the visions reported in the survey. As before, these visions are pleasant and comforting.

> *A male patient at the end stages of cancer spoke about being in a garden filled with flowers and fruit trees. He said it reminded him of his yard at home when the orange trees were in bloom. The experience was peaceful and comforting to the patient and to me for it seemed he was going to heaven. I don't know what heaven looks like but from his description it must be a beautiful place.*

> *A 65 year old male saw a beautiful farm like where he grew up filled with green fields and bright lights from above. He asked if he could go there, if it was alright to leave. I told him to go. I said he was allowed to leave if he wanted. He died 15 minutes later. He had said that he could feel the wind on his face. There was no wind in the room.*

My mother said my aunt told her of a large white porch filled with beautiful fragrant flowers and a yard of flowers too beautiful to describe.

A female patient saw deceased family members and spoke with them. The patient stated that her family told her it was not her time yet and that everything was beautiful. She described white apartment like homes with all her family together. She described beautiful, colorful lights. This experience comforted the patient and myself.

The following is a story about a garden and how the patient knew that what she saw meant she would be dying soon. It also is a demonstration of how coherent and lucid the dying can be. Indeed, a primary difference between DBVs and NDEs is that in the DBV the patient is conscious and alert.

There was this 54 year old patient that spoke of a beautiful place filled with roses and lots of butterflies made of bright lights. She reached up from her bed and told me she was trying to catch the butterflies. When I asked her if she could show me the butterflies she got a very serious look on her face and told me, "It's not your time yet dear. When you are ready to go you'll see the butterflies". She died later that day on my shift, but I'll never forget how she spoke about those butterflies.

The following is an example of a patient not expected to die, yet knowing her time was near.

Early out of nursing school an elderly lady was sent for a procedure. She was not acutely ill at the time but when she returned from the test she was very weak and "washed out". She was placed on the commode. When I entered again, she was looking shocky and said, "I see the pearly gates". She then went unresponsive, coded and died. I believe she saw what she stated." But her death was unexpected.

Sometimes the gardens or beautiful places are a backdrop to reunions with deceased family members.

A male patient, I had years ago, spoke of seeing his loved ones in a garden. He told me there was a peaceful feeling of wanting to go and not stay on this earth associated with the garden.

Deathbed experiences can come in any combination of people, places or things such as deceased relatives, pets, religious figures and gardens. They all seem meant to ease the dying process for the patient.

A 76 year old man had been speaking to his dead parents on and off for days. Then one afternoon he turned to me and smiled looking so peaceful. He looked up at the ceiling and said, "I'm coming. This place is so beautiful with all the lights and clouds everywhere." Then he died.

I had a 60 year old patient who before he died spoke of a light which led to a beautiful, peaceful field.

One of the nurses in the survey, affected by the visions of beautiful places and things, summarized her views as follows:

> *I don't know what she (the patient) saw, but I
> sure hope one day I get to see it too.*

Chapter 5: Comforting Chronicles

"Come softly, darling, come softly to me"
Lyrics by Bob Welch

The common thread that weaves through the vast majority of these stories is that both the dying and the living find these experiences comforting. In the survey, 87% of the nurses reported that the event was spiritually moving and/or comforting for them. They reported that families felt relieved to know that their loved one was not going to be alone in transition. Many nurses reported the visions were spiritual experiences for them and that they felt God was nearby at these times. When asked whether they felt these visions were spiritual or hallucinatory experiences, 85% were of the opinion that they were spiritual experiences with only 15% believing they were hallucinations of the dying mind. Below are some stories that reinforce the comforting nature of these experiences.

> *An 83 year old man was dying and saw a policeman dressed in white and riding a white horse. The patient was comforted by the belief that this was an angel waiting to take his soul to heaven. I also found myself very comforted by this.*

> *When my grandmother died she spoke of seeing white horses and lights. This was very comforting for me because I knew my grandmother would be going to heaven and was spiritually ready to cross over.*

> *I had a female patient who was almost in a state of ecstasy toward the end. The comfort and peace*

that she found had a very positive impact on me as well.

There was an elderly woman in a nursing home who had not spoken in years. She was overheard comforting a woman whose mother had just died in the room next to hers. She said," It's alright; the man with wings is in your mother's room right now." The daughter was so struck by this that she contacted the family of the woman to ask them about her comment. Her family came out to the nursing home and questioned those who had heard the comment. They just could not believe she spoke. She never spoke again and died six months later without saying another word.

Family members of patients speak to me about visions seen by their loved ones. Mostly, they see relatives and bright lights. Sometimes they see figures without a face or someone they do not recognize. Sometimes they talk about seeing children playing or beautiful gardens. In my experience, the patients have been comforted and at ease with their visions. I find that most of these visions occur only once. If it does reoccur, it is just before death.

Chapter 6: Silent Deathbed Visions

"Death is no more than passing from one room to another
but there is a difference for me, you know,
because in that other room, I shall be able to see."
Helen Keller, author and activist

One does not have to have vision to have these deathbed experiences. Many who are blind also share in these phenomena which are referred to as silent DBVs. In these circumstances, it is the dying's non-verbal communication that can alert you to what they are experiencing.

> *A 91 year old blind female opened her eyes, looked around the room as if she were following something up on the ceiling. She was smiling during this time. She did this for 15 minutes before she died.*
>
> *I was at the bedside of a 16 year old girl dying of a brain tumor. She was bedridden, blind and could no longer speak. She was, however, very alert and could sign into her father's hand. I was at her bedside asking her if she was in pain (no) or needed medication for restlessness (no). She kept signing rapidly. She then smiled and signed that her grandmother, who was deceased, was sitting at the foot of her bed. She signed that her grandmother told her that she would follow her soon and that she should not be afraid. Her parents and I cried. We told her she would not be alone. She died peacefully the next morning.*

In these accounts, there is no information about how

long the patients had been blind or whether they had been blind since birth. Assessing what the blind "see" has been an intriguing and controversial area of investigation in the field of NDE research.[1, 2, and 3] Just when the definitive case seems to have appeared, it later is found to be a composite picture of several patients or the claims are unverifiable. The questions in these cases under investigation are also relevant to DBVs. Are those who have been blind since birth able to see visions? A person who previously had normal vision for some part of his or her life might be expected to have some residual normal imagery, but what about those who never had vision? Kenneth Ring, PhD, the leading researcher in this area, has found that some congenitally blind patients had vision in their NDEs, but had never previously reported experiencing visual images in their dreams. He postulates that these individuals who "see" in their NDEs might have access to some "expanded supersensory awareness." He further suggests that people who experience NDEs as well as Out-of-Body Experiences (OBEs) enter a transcendental state that he calls "mindsight."

An Out-of-Body Experience (OBE) is not only a near death phenomenon, it can occur at various times to anyone. In an OBE, people have a sensation of separating from their bodies and viewing events and details that are happening below them. During NDEs some blind individuals have had OBEs and have been able to report on events with some accuracy.[4] These experiences are referred to as veridical NDEs since they can be validated by others. To date, it has been difficult to find individuals who meet the criteria of being blind since birth, having an NDE and it being a verifiable event. Part of the difficulty has been that much of the data in this area has been anecdotal. There are, however, some cases that appear to meet these criteria, but have been difficult or impossible to corroborate. Research continues in this area. Extending this research to include DBVs might add to the data of what the blind "see" prior to death. At the current writing, nothing can be found about this area of investigation pertaining to DBVs.

Another area related to vision involves "the Stare." Nurses and hospice workers are well aware of the "stare." They know that death can not be far behind when patients exhibit this behavior.

> *A 49 year old paraplegic was dying with me and his family in the room. He began to stare into the corner of the ceiling. He mouthed some words to himself. He looked very peaceful and calm. He nodded and then died.*

The dying patient at times will use silent gestures to indicate that there is someone with them.

> *A 92 yr old female was dying of Congestive Heart Failure. Very shortly before she died, she began picking at the air and reaching out to something or someone. She smiled relaxed and died.*

> *One of my patients put her hand out in front of her as if to connect physically with a vision. When she did so, her faced brightened and she had an expression of peace.*

Chapter 7: Other Types of Visions

"I shall hear in heaven."
Ludwig Von Beethoven, composer

The beauty of these deathbed experiences is not only experienced through our "sight" but also through other senses. Other Visions is a category that includes everything that falls outside of the major visions of dead relatives, Jesus, angels and beautiful places. These visions constituted 11% of the stories reported. They included reports of heavenly music or choirs, patients hearing messages but not seeing a vision, bright lights, as well as strange experiences witnessed by staff members at the time of the patient's death.

Bright lights are one of the hallmarks of the near death experience and can be seen in deathbed visions as well. Bright lights are the most common type of "other" visions appearing in the survey. In the following stories, patients describe such lights prior to the moment of death.

The first vision I ever experienced came early in my nursing career. The patient said there was a bright light and she wanted to go to the light. She said the light made her feel peaceful and happy. She died right after that.

An elderly female had been slowly dying of a bad heart and had been very weak for several days. One day she sat up and opened her eyes and said, "The lights are so...beautiful". Her family had been at her bedside at the time and they told the older woman to go to the lights. They told her they wanted her to go. She did and died a few moments later.

A lady in her 70's was dying very peacefully. She said that she saw a bright, white, warm light. She had a contented look on her face. I wasn't sure at the time how this affected me since I was comfortable with the situation. Now I feel it helped me to be more comfortable with the dying experience.

My most moving experience happened on the Oncology floor with a lady in her 80's who knew she was dying of cancer. She was on several medications for pain but had not reported any hallucinations. She called me to her bedside and asked "Do you see the light?" She pointed to the ceiling of the room. I, of course, did not see anything but I validated her experience believing that she did see something. The patient asked me to pray with her which I did. When the prayers were over, I went about my other duties. When I returned to check on her she had died.

A dying female patient stated, "They are coming for me. I see the bright lights."

A religious, 79 year old male was always speaking to the Lord and talking about the bright lights around him. His family just thought he was delirious and paid him no mind. Then one day he turned to them and smiled. "I'll send you a sign and then you'll know what I'm telling you is true." He died that day and the family later reported back to me that a rainbow had appeared over the man's house the very same moment he died.[1]

Another elderly male spoke of seeing someone in his room and told me of how wonderful, precious and sweet the "bright person" was. He lifted his hands to the ceiling, smiled and said "They are ready to go." Within a few hours he was dead.

———————◆◆◆———————

Heavenly choirs or unusual music also appear here. The dying told of hearing distant music playing or hearing singing that could not be explained.

I had a 90 year old patient who spoke numerous times of hearing a beautiful choir singing and the brushing of angel wings. When she spoke of these things she became calm, peaceful and smiled.

I had this one male patient when I worked in ICU. He was recovering from a heart attack and was doing very well; in fact he was to be discharged the next day. He called me to his bedside and stated, "Do you hear that?" I thought perhaps the patient was talking about the monitor above his bed or some other noise in the room. "Do you hear the singing?" he asked. I immediately looked up at the monitors thinking the patient was having some medical problem but all was well. I asked him what kind of singing he heard and he told me about some beautiful choir, not a choir but strange very lyrical voices, unlike any choir he had ever heard. I thought maybe his ears were ringing due to too much medicine. I assured him that it was probably just the meds he was on affecting his hearing and I left the room. Fifteen minutes later he called me back to his bedside. "They're getting louder," he said. A few seconds later his heart stopped and we never got him back. I always wondered about that choir he heard. I've always remembered that experience.

———◆◆◆———

One nurse has been able to use her knowledge of this phenomenon to help prepare her in working with other patients.

> *I have had a few patients who have heard harps playing right before they died. Now when any patient tells me that I know what to expect."*

———◆◆◆———

Just as in the previous chapter, when patients "knew" the time of their death, other patients have knowledge of events that they seemingly should not know. These experiences are frequently interpreted as being associated with Extrasensory Perception (ESP). Indeed, Osis and Haroldsson[2] claim that deathbed visions are extrasensory perceptions of the afterlife. The following story is just such an example.

> *A 58 year old man was dying and he told me that his daughter was pregnant and going to have a baby girl named Michelle. Later that day when I saw the man's daughter I congratulated her on the new arrival. She looked at me as if I was crazy. I found out the woman was not pregnant and then I began to tell her what her father had said to me. We both went into the patient's room to confront him about this weird news. When the daughter asked the man about his fantasy, he told her that it would come true soon. The voices had told him about her pregnancy. He said they had told him that so he knew it would be all right to leave his daughter. A week later the man died. Three weeks later his daughter called me out of the blue. She was pregnant. Nine months later she had a baby girl named Michelle.*

Many times the dying patients have important messages for the nurse too.

> *I have had at least two or three patients tell me to live a "good life" and then die. It was the same message over and over again to live a "good life" before I die. I always got the impression they were trying to pass on some vital bit of information before they moved on.*

Chapter 8: Distressing Deathbed Visions

"I am in flames!"
Dying words of David Hume, philosopher and atheist

This current chapter suggests that there may be a good reason for the dying to tell others to live a good life. In the previous chapters, the majority of deathbed experiences appear to be overwhelmingly positive for the patient, the family and the healthcare provider. Popular books on the subject for the public to date tend to report only positive experiences. In this survey, not all of the experiences can be described as pleasant. Indeed some of the stories are quite nightmarish, as can be seen in the following examples:

> *A female on her deathbed was screaming and gripping my hand. She said she saw an evil being coming to get her and she was afraid to be alone. She was terrified and tried to climb under the bed to escape. It was distressing to watch and I was unable to offer anything to comfort her.*

> *A man lying on his bed dying of cancer began gripping the hand of the family member next to him and began to yell, "Don't let them take me." Believing in life after death, his last words bothered me for a long time. I always thought that people would welcome the crossing over, unless for some reason they were not going to a good place. I have always felt sad about his last words because in my mind he wasn't going to a good place.*

> *A middle age woman was said to have been*

completely lucid. Suddenly, she began yelling for someone to come help her. She was yelling at us to get "that thing" away from her and there was nothing in the room. She was frantic. She kept saying that "it" was coming to get her and that "it" was getting closer. Finally she began yelling that "it" was on her chest. She was screaming, went into V-tach and died. That obviously affected me in a negative way as it was quite frightening.

A female in her mid 20's yelled and screamed, "No, no I don't want to go."

Another patient of mine began writhing and moaning in her bed and kept saying, "I need to get away."

A man close to dying started yelling out, "It's hot, Oh no, it's hot."

My first hospice patient to die was just a few years older than me. We had spoken on admission about getting things in order. The doctors had told me she only had a few days to live. She was in denial, although her platelets dropped dramatically with each infusion. A week later, on a Sunday morning I was called by her son. On arrival, it was evident she was actively dying. She was still talking at times. When she would moan, I gave her pain meds. After a couple of hours, she had definitely declined. Her five children, mother and sister were at her bedside. She sat straight up in the bed and said "Where is the fire? I smell the smoke" and she collapsed back on the bed. A few minutes later, she sat up in the bed and said "Get those things off my legs" and was rubbing her legs. The last thing she said to me was "I waited too long" and then she died.

Nurses who were witness to these experiences found them uncomfortable and frightening. One nurse related several experiences in which patients stated that they were in their tombs. She found these to be eerie and frightening. The nurses seemed to be troubled the most by the fact that there was nothing they could do to help ease the patients' fears and comfort them. While we have no anecdotal information regarding the effect of this on family members, one can only imagine what that experience would be like for them.

Another nurse related an experience that was horrifying for her and the patient. The patient did not die, but the nurse's inability to console him was a source of deep distress.

> *A man in his sixties was having a myocardial infarction (MI) and frequent runs of ventricular tachycardia (VTs) which are periods of being without a pulse. When in V-tach, he began having flashbacks of dropping bombs on Germany in WWII. He would come out of V-tach periods crying and screaming and telling me about the images that he saw. I stayed with him and held his hand and desperately tried to stop the VTs.*

Dr. Elizabeth Kubler-Ross, the twentieth century ground-breaker in the study of death and dying, said that we are never alone when we die.[1] It appears as though not all who come to take us away are of a benevolent nature. Osis and Haroldsson [2] in their book, *At the Hour of Death*, report that some of the patients in their cross-cultural study reported that some take-away visions were experienced as frightening. They found that only one person in the American survey found the take-away vision distressing while about one-third of the East Indian population resisted being taken away. The authors suggest that the Indians' resistance to dying is based on Indian mythology. In the Indian tradition, Yama is the King of Death. His messengers are the Yamdoots. When a Yamdoot appears at the bedside of someone dying, the patient's Karma is said to determine whether the figure will be pleasant or frightful. In these latter cases, it was reported the Yamdoots were seen as frightening and the individual did not want to go with them. Negative personifications of death such as the Grim Reaper did not appear in the American sample nor were they reported in these stories.

A basic tenet in all religions is that if you live a good life, you go to heaven or paradise. If you have not led a good life, you will go to some form of Hell. Christian belief about the afterlife varies somewhat depending on the particular denomination as well as the person's individual belief. The vast majority of Christians believe in some type of Heaven and Hell. In addition, Catholics believe in Purgatory. In the Koran (4:59/60),[3] it states that those who believe and do good deeds will be admitted to Paradise while those who have not lived in accordance with these tenets go to "the fire." In Judaism, there is a full range of religious expression about the afterlife found in the Reform, Conservative, and the Orthodox movements. These beliefs range from a focus on earthly life and deeds to a belief in the afterlife and reincarnation. In Judaism, no one belief has ever been officially established.

In the *Tibetan Book of Living and Dying*,[4] it is said that we begin to have visions at the time of our dying. If there has been a lot of negativity in our lives, we may see terrifying forms and have frightening experiences based on our past deeds. If our lives have been filled with caring and compassion, then we are likely to see our loved ones and religious figures as we transition. For those who have led good lives there is peace at death and not fear. Perhaps the woman in an earlier story knew what she was talking about when she told the nurse to be sure and live a good life.

There are numerous parallels in the views of dying and the afterlife between the Tibetan Buddhists and the Jewish tradition especially as found in the Kabballistic teachings. Kabballah is the system of Jewish teachings about God based on mystical insight. The *Zohar* is derived from the Kabballah and is the mystical commentary on the Torah. It is perhaps the most important work for understanding the afterlife teachings in Judaism. The Zohar refers to angelic beings, guides, deceased relatives and even some demonic figures that come at the time of our death. [5] Authors [6, 7, 8] agree that the specific content of what we see is largely determined by cultural and religious beliefs. In terms of religious beliefs, Christians are likely to see Christ, but Catholics may also see Mary or a saint. Buddhists will see The Buddha. Jews are likely to see angels. Of course, this is not always the situation. Many are surprised by whom they see. In Greyson and Bush's[9] article on distressing near death experiences, they give the example of a Jewish woman having a near death experience and seeing Jesus. It seems as though we should be prepared for whoever comes to meet us.

Having a distressing experience at the time of death has been the primary focus of research on Near Death Experiences (NDEs). In earlier times, frightening deathbed visions were demonstrated in the symbolism and art of Christians and Hindus. Encounters with evil forces and other horrors were depicted. Even the Being of Light as shown in the *Tibetan Book of the Dead* is seen as terrifying.[10] Evangelical Christian scholars quote the bible[11] (2 Corinthians 11:14) in their claim that the figure of light is actually Satan in disguise. While NDE's have been referenced since biblical times, it seems to have only been since the mid 1980's and early 1990's that current distressing experiences were "discovered" and investigation into these experiences began. Prior to that time, when information about NDE's began to surface as a result of Raymond Moody's book, *Life After Life*, [12] the only experiences that were reported were of a positive nature, just as has been the case in the early literature on DBVs. However, is it that these distressing experiences are rare happenings or is it that people do not want to discuss them with others? It is easy for people to accept the positive experiences as spiritual events but when confronted with a distressing experience, they are quick to say that "it must be their medication" or they are just "hallucinating." Our reactions to these distressing experiences reflect our own fears of death and the unknown. No one really wants to believe that it is possible to go to Hell at death. On hearing about distressing experiences, people are also perhaps too quick to assume that the individual has been "bad" or led an "evil" life. Atwater [13] states, at least in her experience with NDEs, that there is no evidence to suggest that frightening experiences are linked with "bad" people. Other researchers, [14, 15] have concluded that everyone has the same potential to experience a distressing NDE. Rommer, who refers to these experiences as Less-Than-Positive (LTP), suggests that there are three reasons why this type of NDE occurs. The first is that it provides an opportunity to reevaluate the person's life, choices and beliefs. They are given another chance to "get it right." The second is said to occur because the person's mindset immediately prior to the event was negative. Finally, she posits that the LTP event occurs due to negative programming as a child. However, it is not known if these apply to distressing DBV's.

Eugene d'Aquili and Andrew Newberg, researchers

on the relationship between the brain and religious experience, address the issue of negative NDEs in their book, *The Mystical Mind.* They state that negative NDEs likely occur with more frequency than reported, but are often downplayed for many different reasons including the patient's not wanting to be judged negatively by others.[16] In medieval times, there was more of a focus on the distressing NDE, although there was acknowledgement of the positive experiences as well. During that time period, people were concerned with morality and used these fearful situations to encourage people to lead a moral life. Today, the emphasis is typically only on the "good" experiences due to our cultures focusing on more positive outcomes.[17] While these negative or distressing experiences clearly happen in both DBVs and NDEs, they do not prove that Hell exists; just as the positive experiences cannot be taken as definitive proof of a Heaven. While there has been investigation into distressing NDEs, disturbing DBVs are often not mentioned and have only recently become of more interest to researchers.

Cardiologist Maurice Rawlings [18] has worked with patients experiencing cardiac arrest and has been there to interview them immediately on being revived. He states that half of his NDE patients had "hellish" experiences leading him to believe that these indeed prove that there is a Hell. He suggests that all NDEs may begin with negative experiences and as they progress become more positive. The frightening experiences are then suppressed.[19]

An example of a distressing NDE is found in Howard Storm's book, *My Descent into Death.*[20] While visiting in Paris, Storm experienced a perforation in his duodenum. He was rushed to the hospital where there was only one surgeon in attendance. While waiting, Storm was in excruciating pain. He was too weak to hang on to life.

In his "death," Storm describes a terrifying situation in which he was being attacked and devoured by evil beings. His experience shifted when he heard a voice telling him to pray. When he prayed, his surroundings changed and he found himself embraced by a luminous being. What followed was a life affirming experience for him. After his recovery, Storm devoted his life to the Christian ministry. Indeed, the majority of those who come back from the brink of death use this experience to change their lives to a more positive direction. We obviously cannot know what happens to those whose death is final.

Four types of distressing NDEs have been identified.[15] The most common type is the typical NDE that is misinterpreted by the person due to feeling out of control of the events. The second type is experiencing a void of emptiness with feelings of utter despair. Howard Storm experienced the third and one of the rarest types of NDE in which the person experiences hellish imagery, such as foreboding landscapes, demonic beings and seeing others in extreme distress. The final type is one in which the individual feels negatively judged by a Higher Power and re-experiences the pain he has caused in this life.

ADDRESSING THE DISTRESSING DBV

From these stories, death does appear to have a "double face" and "promises both suffering and bliss" for us all.[17] When distressing experiences at death do occur, they disturb and frighten all involved. A nurse I knew described a situation to me in which she was working with a nurse from a different culture. When the dying patient began to talk about what he was experiencing, the foreign nurse ran out of the room screaming. This is not a good thing for the patient or the nurse. The problem in these situations is that we really have no definitive answers for these disturbing experiences. If people are reluctant to talk about death, they are certainly not inclined to discuss distressing death-bed visions. Given the relative paucity of information on these negative experiences, how are we to understand them? More importantly, how do we explain them to the family? Perhaps the best way is to acknowledge the person's distress and tell them these are not uncommon experiences and that those who have come back from a distressing experience report that it ultimately shifted to a pleasant, spiritual encounter. It is important during this time not to be judgmental or to label the event, regardless of what your thoughts and beliefs may be. The importance of helping the family by soothing and comforting them at this time cannot be overstated. The remainder of their lives could be negatively impacted by their loved one's disturbing passing and their own interpretation of the events. In listening to family members whose loved one has had a distressing experience, they are not only frightened but angry and confused that their loved one did not have a "good death." Nurses are in a unique position to offer support and understanding. Perhaps as more research is conducted in this area, other information will be available and provide additional explanations to help the dying and their families have a more peaceful transition.

Chapter 9: Near Death Experiences

"Suddenly thousands of angels surrounded me. They were exuberant, that I had made the decision to return."
Betty J. Eadie, author[1]

In the previous chapter, there was a major focus on NDE's, where the majority of the comparable research to DBVs has been done. Raymond Moody, in his groundbreaking work *Life After Life* [2] identified three different categories of death-related experiences. Two had to do with near-death experiences and the third was about the experiences of those who, as they died, told their visions to others who were present at the time. Moody states that he made a decision to focus on the near death experiences to make the data easier to manage and to be able to use first hand reports. As a result of his book, there has been a wealth of information collected over the years about NDEs.[3] Very little attention, however, has been given to DBVs. It is as though DBVs have been the stepchild of research on the dying experience. According to the International Association of Near Death Studies (IANDS), there are now chapters located in all parts of the world with researchers, those who have experienced an NDE and family members all come together for support and to explore these phenomena.

Moody has identified at least 15 elements that can occur in an NDE. They are as follows: difficulty finding the words to capture the experience; (2) hearing the news of the death; (3) feelings of peace and calm; (4) unusual noises that can range from a whirring sound to beautiful music; (5) the dark tunnel; (6) finding yourself out of your body; (7)

meeting others such as family and/or spiritual beings; (8) the Being of Light; (9) the life review; (10) the border or limit reached before being returned to your body; (11) coming back to your body; (12) telling others about the experience; (13) positive effects on the lives of the experiencer; (14) new views of death, and (15) corroboration of the event from others. It should be noted that seldom are all the above present in any one NDE. Non-Western NDE research has been conducted in China, Thailand, Tibet, and India as well as in some native cultures such as in Australia, Hawaii, and Guam. Findings indicate common elements among the cultures. Individuals felt that they were experiencing the afterlife. There was a profound sense of otherworldly peace and meetings with deceased relatives and religious figures. The tunnel sensation, however, was rarely reported in non-western cultures. For example in Japan, physicians in Kyorin spent a year studying 17 patients who had been in comas and were resuscitated. Instead of going through a tunnel, these individuals reported walking through ponds and reservoirs.[4] Chinese Taoist believe that after death, the soul crosses a bridge to the next life. It appears that while the conveyances may be different, there is some form of crossing over/passing through involved in all cultures.

Kenneth Ring developed an index to measure the most frequently occurring NDE experiences and found 5 aspects. These include: peace, body separation, entering the darkness, seeing the Light, and entering the Light. In the following stories, you will see many of these elements. Many of the nurses were kind enough to share experiences of their own relatives who experienced NDEs. Some also shared their own personal NDEs. All the stories that were received were of a positive nature.

> *As a teenager, I was severely ill in the hospital*
> *and had received last rites. One night the figure*
> *of Jesus was at my door. I asked him not to take*

me yet. We talked. I bargained at first and then became overwhelmingly peaceful and unafraid. I wanted to go with him. Bright lights filled the room. The next morning I awoke surprised to find myself still alive. It was this experience that made me want to become a nurse so I could help heal others.

This is another experience in which the individual came back to live a life of service to others.

A 60 year old male coded in the hospital. When he was revived he described it as a peaceful moment from which he had not wanted to leave. He stated that he wanted to go back. He said "You brought me back this time but next time, I will not come back." Ninety minutes later he died.

A five year old boy was undergoing surgery when he coded. He was defibrillated twice before he returned to a normal sinus rhythm. He was then sent to the ICU. Because of his age, the staff and his family did not tell him what had happened during the surgery. When his grandmother came to visit, the young boy told her that he had seen his grandfather during the surgery. His grandfather had died six months previously. The young boy also told his grandmother that before seeing his grandfather he had been afraid of dying in surgery.

I was extremely ill and was a no-code, meaning that they were to take no measures to revive me if I began to die. I had lost 95% of the functioning of a vital organ. On dying, I remember people coming to talk to me. They were people who had died and sometimes people that I did not know. Once I was in a tunnel and there was a beautiful white light that glowed from the end of the tunnel. I never reached the end of the tunnel because I kept being sent back. I am healed now and have been able to return to nursing.

A patient in the ICU suffered a cardiac arrest and was intubated, sedated and ventilated for 24 hours. As soon as he was extubated the next day, he immediately began to tell me about his walk along a long white fence toward a bright light. He wanted desperately to go to the light. However, he knew that if he did, he would die. He believed that his wife and children were not prepared for life without him. He made a decision to walk back along the white fence toward life.

A male patient was admitted to the hospital in full cardiac arrest. Resuscitation had been going on for an hour before he arrived on the unit. The patient was unresponsive and was shocked (cardioverted) several times. I worked night shift and the patient had come in at the end of my shift. When I returned the following day, the patient had been intubated again but kept trying to say something to me. I could not understand him as he was still intubated He wrote and said "I watched you from the ceiling. Thank you for everything."

Complications developed with a cardiac procedure. On awakening, the patient said that he had seen a tunnel with a very bright light and that everything was very calm.

A 14 year old male had a medical procedure done and on his third day post-op he developed serious complications. He was transferred to an ICU and the family was told that he would probably die. He was intubated for ten days and against all odds, he began to recover. When he was able to speak, he shared three things with his mother. The first was that her great grandfather was holding his head for awhile and had saved him from having it cut off. When asked how he knew it was her great grandfather, the young man said that he had told him so. He then proceeded to describe him in detail. On his return home, he was able to identify him from a picture that he had never seen before. The boy also told his mother that he was aware that he almost died, but did not seem upset by this. He stated that he had a vision of being drawn to a garden, a beautiful garden with a fence around it. He opened a gate to go inside but a man's voice told him to stop. The voice gave him a choice to come inside the garden which he knew would mean his death. The voice told him that it was his choice but that they were really not ready for him. He told his mom that he returned on his own.

The last experience he shared with his mother was about his grandmother's boyfriend, Mr. Sam, who had died one month prior to the onset of his illness. The two of them had been very close. One morning when his mom came to visit, she sat in the chair next to his bed. Her son looked at her and said that it was a good thing she had come late because she would have sat on Mr. Sam's lap. He told her that he had trouble sleeping the night before and that Mr. Sam had been sitting by his bed all night talking to him, telling him he was going to get better. He told him he would have a long road ahead of him but that he was going to be OK. He repeated to him that they were not ready for him in heaven.

It seems that even when we are not transitioning, our loved ones come to soothe and reassure us. Help is all around us.

Family members and I were gathered around the bed of a dying man. He had asked that all members of the family be there. His son, however, was on route when he died. Afterwards, they prepared his body for pick up. His wife commented that the one thing he asked God for was that the entire family be present. The wife was grieving that her son had not been there. Fifteen or twenty minutes passed. His extremities were blue and molten. The patient took a deep breath and called out for his son. His wife had called the son on her cell phone prior to this. She gave the phone to him and he told his son goodbye. At that time the room was filled with a radiant light. The man then gave the phone back to his wife. She kissed him and he died again. This time he did not return.

I had two daughters and was expecting my third. I went into labor at four months and found out I had a tumor. During surgery, my soul came out of my body after they put me to sleep. I hovered over the body watching them as they worked. After surgery, I was brought to a room and left there. I began to hemorrhage. I realized that I was being drawn through a tunnel and when I stopped, I was in a city bustling with activity. A man in a small station told me that I had the choice to stay or go back. It was not said in words but in understanding. Next, I began to see an immediate review of my life from childhood till that moment. I told them that I did not want to go back. It was too painful. Then he asked me what I had not done. I answered that I had not yet taught my children to love. I was then immediately drawn back into my body. It was like entering a wetsuit in winter. It was difficult to take a breath. My body was cold. I could see them trying to arouse me. I was taken back into surgery. The following afternoon, I was discharged totally well. This experience had such a profound effect on me that I entered nursing and have spent my career in hospice work helping others.

A man was having a cardiac procedure when complications developed. He said that he woke up and sat up. Someone pushed him down. He said that next he saw a tunnel with a very bright light. He said everything was very calm. Before seeing the bright light, there was lots of noise and shouting and then no noise.

Chapter 10: Dreams

"I'll see you in my dreams."
Isham Jones, composer and Gus Kahn, lyricist

Pre-death visions not only come when the dying are awake, but may also come in the form of dreams. In *Dreaming Beyond Death* by Bulkeley and Bulkley, [1] the authors talk about pre-death dreams and their ability to help prepare one for the end of life. The dreams appear to be helpful in lessening the fear of death. Rosalind Cartwright in *Crises Dreaming* [2] states that in addition to easing the fear of death, dreams help prepare us for the end, enable us to say our goodbyes, and help strengthen ties with our loved ones. Two of the most prevalent themes that appear in pre-death dreams are very similar to those in deathbed visions. These are (1) death as a journey and (2) the meeting of a guide, who may be a family member who has died, a religious figure, or a spiritual figure. These are very similar to the content that was found in the deathbed visions. Three pre-death dreams were described in the survey and are listed below.

> *A woman in her 70's shared her dreams with me. She told me of seeing her dead son and other relatives that had died years ago. She was discharged home and seemed relatively healthy at the time. She died a few weeks later. I felt that her dreams were preparing her for dying.*

> *A 98 year old woman stated that she was asleep and dreaming; God woke her up at 4:00am. He told her that he was taking her daughter and would be coming back for her. The next day, her 72 year old daughter died from ovarian cancer. When the family gathered*

to tell her that her daughter was dead, she told them that she already knew because God had told her.

A very young patient that I became very close to had a running joke about cruising the halls for good looking men. When she was at the very end of her life, she told me that the night before in a dream, she was on the beach and a very good looking lifeguard had come to rescue her. She could not tell me what he looked like specifically because the sun was glowing around his face. She smiled and said he was all hers. Within the next few hours, she was gone. I have since then believed that he was her angel. Because she was smiling at the time, I no longer believe death is dark and somber.

Just as there are pre-death dreams and pre-death visions in which deceased family members come to prepare us for transition, there are also dreams in which they return to us after death to help us heal from our grief. Long after they are gone, our loved ones are with us in our dreams. According to Garfield, [3] dreams of the dead tend to vary based on the mourners stage of grieving, length of time of loss, the type of death and our relationship with the deceased. Guggenheim and Guggenheim[4] refer to these experiences as "sleep state after death communications." Wray and Price[5] in their book *Grief Dreams* identify the four most common grief dreams: (1) visitation dreams, (2) message dreams, (3) reassurance dreams and (4) trauma dreams. Visitation dreams are those in which the deceased usually comes back to let us know they are all right. Message dreams are those in which they tell us something, give us information, or warn us. Reassurance dreams serve to console and comfort those left behind. Finally, the trauma dreams are so named because they traumatize the dreamer. These are nightmares involving the dead. The authors state that these dreams are meant to facilitate healing and to help us deal with the pain of our loss. While our survey was about deathbed visions, several respondents reported dreams that had elements of visitation, reassurance and messages.

> *After my mother-in law's death, my father-in- law experienced a dream in which she appeared to him. As he reached out to touch her, she told him not to touch her since she had not yet seen the "Father." She told him she was alright and not to worry. She also told him how much she loved him.*[6]

> *Three days after my mother died, she appeared to me in a dream. I was in nursing school at the time and had made an A in a class. She came to me in a dream and hugged me. She told me she knew that I had done well on my paper and that she would always be proud of me. Another time more recently, I awoke on my birthday and felt completely surrounded by her and her love.*

> *I had been privy to many of my mother's death bed visions. After she died, I waited, not too patiently, to receive a message from her. Finally one night, she contacted me by phone in my dream. She had "called" to say that she was alright. The dream woke me up. I was so happy to hear from her and to know that she was alright.*

> *My father had died very suddenly when I was 13. The last time I saw him was when the EMT's placed him on the gurney to put him in the ambulance. My father died shortly after arriving at the hospital. At that time, I knew nothing about death, and certainly never expected to dream about it. Shortly after the funeral, I recall the*

worst nightmare I had ever experienced. I cried for days and was inconsolable. It was quite awhile before I could even share it with my mother. In the dream, I was in the room where my father was dying. He was on the gurney. There were many other people in the room with me and my father and they were gathered all around him. Somehow I knew that these were all relatives that had previously died. The figure of death was also there. When I discussed it with my mother, it helped to talk about it but I never forgot the dream. As an adult working with the dying I eventually came to understand the meaning of the dream. I came to realize that these were spirits who had come to escort my father home on the day he died. Years later, the dream finally had brought me peace and comfort.

Finally, a nurse told me of a dream that a physician shared with her that was a turning point in his life. He was a cat lover. His favorite cat had disappeared. He loved that cat and worried about what had happened to her. Six weeks after her disappearance, he had a dream that changed his life. She came to him and communicated that he no longer needed to worry about her because she was alright. Shortly after this dream, he received a phone call from some boys in the neighborhood. They had found the cat dead and in the place where he had seen her in the dream. The dream had a profound effect on him in many different ways. He had always been a "non-believer" when it came to spirituality and psychic type experiences. The dream opened his mind to the idea that there is more to life than what our five senses tell us. In his professional life, the physician became more empathic with his patients

Chapter 10: Dreams

and listened to them without being dismissive when they spoke of "unusual experiences."

Chapter 11: After-Death Communication

"I do not believe in an after life, although I am bringing a change of underwear."
Woody Allen, comedian

Dreams are not the only form that after-death communications (ADC) can take. Indeed, the most common ADC is the deathbed vision. This chapter is different from the previous ones in that the accounts are not from the nurses but from information I have been privileged to hear over the years. They have been included to complete the known spectrum of death-related phenomena.

Typically ADCs are spontaneous and direct with no third party such as a medium involved. While it is not uncommon for the bereaved to seek out psychics or mediums, a direct communication from their loved one tends to be the most powerful and satisfying. People are more likely to talk about these experiences now than in the past. But there is still some hesitancy involved due to the fear of being ridiculed. After-death communications can be fleeting or lengthy. They can happen once or many times. Contact can occur immediately after death or years later. ADCs can be experienced by both children and adults. Regardless of the circumstances, the purpose of these contacts is to comfort and reassure the bereaved. The importance of these events cannot be measured. They provide hope and can lift mourners out of their despair.

In 1985, a groundbreaking book was written by Guggenheim and Guggenheim, titled *Hello From Heaven*.[1] In it, twelve of the most frequent types of ADC's were identified. On reading about them, many have been able to go back and see where their loved one had indeed attempted to communicate with them. Perhaps in reading these descriptions listed below, you too, may become aware of having had such an experience.

Sensing a Presence: The most common type of ADC reported is feeling the presence of a loved one. This is described as a specific physical sensation that the loved one is nearby. The bereaved report a feeling of peace and well being during these encounters.

Hearing a Voice: Some people state they hear their loved one's voice as though he or she were in the room. However, most of these communications tend to be experienced through telepathy, "hearing" the voice of the deceased in their minds. Such experiences often may lead to two-way conversations with the deceased.

Feeling a Touch: Individuals may experience the deceased as patting or holding their hand, putting an arm around them or even kissing them. Such physical contacts are the loved one's way of showing comfort, reassurance and affection.

Smelling a Fragrance: Many people report they become aware of an aroma that has been associated with the departed. The fragrance can be of cologne, perfume, or any scent associated with the deceased. Often the smell of flowers is detected with roses being the most frequently mentioned.

Visual Experiences: Seeing visions of the departed are also described and can range from an ephemeral appearance to seeing a more solid form. While these visions can occur at any place or time, they most often are reported to occur in the bedroom, at the foot of the bed. The deceased also can appear in photographs. They can show up as white amorphous figures in a photo or in the form of a radiant color.

Visions: Here the deceased is said to make a lifelike, full body appearance which looks solid and real. In such visions, the deceased appear as healed and whole once again. These images are also frequently described as being in radiant colors. They can be seen with the eyes opened or closed. Their appearance often serves as a sign to the bereaved that the loved one is all right.

Twilight Experiences: Any or all of the above ADCs can occur during altered states of consciousness such as falling asleep, waking up, praying or meditating.

ADCs While Asleep: It seems that the deceased often initiate contact when the bereaved is more relaxed and open to these communications such as during sleep. These sleep-state ADCs are different from regular dreams. In the former, the dreamer usually feels the deceased is with them in person having an actual visit. When these occur, they are described as more intense and real than regular dreams.

Out-of-Body ADCs: Described as one of the more dramatic ADCs is the out-of-body contact with the deceased. These can occur during sleep or meditation and are said to be like visitations with the departed in their new environment. The words used to describe the setting are similar to how the dying report the DBV, beautiful and with intense colors.

Physical Phenomena: There are a wide variety of physical signs that the deceased are thought to use to get our attention and to announce their presence. These may include lights going off and on, objects falling from a shelf, appliances turning on, or items being moved around.

Telephone Calls: These are a frequent form of communication that may occur in either a dream state or while awake. Phones may actually ring. When answered, the voice of the deceased is said to be heard. With cell phones now, it is not unusual to have the deceased's photo appear on the screen.

Symbolic ADCs: A frequent plea of survivors is that their beloved send them a sign or message that they are all right. These signs are said to take many different forms such as feathers, butterflies, flowers, animals or coins. The form that these symbolic signs take vary but they are always meaningful to the recipient.

The following accounts of ADCs illustrate many of the more common elements discussed above. They have been grouped according to the experiences of each person separately. Interestingly, none of the respondents asked for their names to be changed, only that there last names not be used. They saw an opportunity for their experiences to help others and were excited to share their accounts. Without exception, the bereaved found solace through their encounters. The first experience below is my own.

———◆———

> *After my mother died, I would find small, fluffy, white feathers everywhere I went. They showed up in places where you would not expect to find feathers. This went on for the first year after her death. I looked forward to finding them and felt that Mother was telling me she was an "angel" watching over me. Even now when I find a feather, I am excited to know that Mother is still around me. My daughter also received visits from my Mother in the form of butterflies. She said, "My first experience after Grandma died was with a big monarch butterfly that landed on me. It brought me a feeling of peace and I knew it was her." Knowing what this communication meant to my daughter and me, I no longer wait for people in my therapy practice to tell me about these experiences,*

Chapter 11: After-Death Communication

I ask about them early in our work together.

———•◆•———

Alice's 24 year old son, Hiram John, died in a motorcycle accident. Her first dream after his death was a visit to Heaven. Alice said that she walked into a room and immediately saw her deceased brother sitting next to his daughter. She was laying her head on her father's shoulder and he was hugging her. Both were smiling. Alice asked her brother where Hiram John was. She said, "I quickly turned and looked where he was pointing. Hiram John stood up from a bench behind a table. He smiled and I ran into his open arms. It was the most wonderful feeling to be able to hug him." He only said a few words to let her know he was fine. Alice reports that he said to her, "Mom, I know you keep asking for me to return to earth, but I don't want to come back."

After Alice's son's death, pennies kept appearing everywhere she would go. One day when she arrived for her session, there was a penny on my waiting room table. There had never been money there before or since. Alice said, "See, I told you. He is always with me."

On numerous occasions, Alice has received calls on her cell phone. The call displays no number but on answering it, a picture of her son appears. Another phone related experience occurred when a cellular phone company called Alice to confirm that she had ordered a new phone. She told them she had not and asked which phone number had requested a new phone. They said it was requested from her son's phone. Several weeks prior to this, one of her daughter's friends was talking on her pink phone. Alice thought to herself that she would like a new pink phone but never told anyone. Five days before Mother's Day, a package was at her front door containing a new pink phone. She called the phone company and they said that none of her accounts were charged for the new phone. Alice knew that this was her Mother's day present from Hiram John.

Alice related many instances in which circles have appeared in family pictures. When her daughter was married and the family posed for a picture, Alice said that next to her was a beautiful circle exactly where her son would have been if he were still alive. In Disneyland when the family was posing for a photographer, she told them that there was something wrong with her camera. She said that there was a large circle in the picture that she was unable to remove. She then offered to take the picture with the family's camera and the circle was still there. Finally, Alice's daughter told the photographer to just take the picture with the circle in it because "it's only my brother."

Laura and Warren had been married for 31 years when Warren was diagnosed with a brain tumor. Shortly after his death, Laura was in the family room with her son. Warren had been a big University of Georgia fan and had collected many memorabilia over the years. Laura stated that looking at the collection made her very sad and she told her son that she would put them away. At that moment, a stuffed figure of a Georgia player fell off the shelf and landed right next to them as if to say, "No, no." Laura said that at first she was scared. The fan was not on and the stuffed figure had been in place for a number of years. "Warren was sending me a message. I still have the collection in the same spot and can now look at it and have happy memories."

Laura related another incident that occurred while in the car listening to the radio with her daughter. "The song Moon River came on and I started to cry. I told my daughter that had been our special song. The very next song was Tell Laura I Love Her."

Warren use to help Laura with the dishes after dinner and they would use that time to talk about their day. One early summer night after his death, Laura was doing the dishes and felt a strong breeze around her. She looked out the window and saw a large beautiful, white egret staring straight at her. She made a noise and tapped at the window, but the bird stood there looking at her. Laura felt very strongly that the egret was a message from Warren saying hello at their special time.

While walking down the halls of the school where she worked, Laura looked down to find a child's playing card from a game. It was lying face down. On the top of the card in bold letters was the name, WARREN. Laura was never able to locate the game from which it came, but kept the card as a message from Warren.

Finally, about seven years after Warren died, Laura began to wonder if she should take off her wedding ring but did not mention it to anyone. One day her daughter found an inexpensive gold ring with the letter "L" on it. Laura felt that Warren had sent the answer to her question. She took off her wedding *ring and replaced it with the "L" ring.*

———————•◆•———————

Roberta's father was a physician who died in April, 1974. In late summer 1978, her daughter became ill. She was running a high temperature. Roberta had been up with her for almost 48 hours trying to make her comfortable. A friend had come over to help and Roberta went into her bedroom. This was the same room in which her father had died. When she sat on the bed, her father appeared before her and told her he was here now and that Tara would be fine. Within the next 30 minutes, Tara's fever broke.

In 1982, Roberta sold the home where she and her parents had lived. After their death, she and her husband took over the house in order to raise her own family there. Roberta states that she had wanted to be alone her last night in the house. It was sad for her to leave. She states that she was in the large glass walled living room late that night and called out to her father, "Daddy, can you give me a sign that you are here?" All the lights went out in the house but not in the neighborhood. "I really believe this was a sign from him."

Roberta had asked her mother for a loan but her mother had turned her down. After her mother's death, she went to see a psychic. During the reading, Roberta was told that her mother was not able to move on due to some unfinished business between them. Roberta did not know what this could be. Two days later her brother found a $10,000 CD. The exact amount the loan would have been.[2]

———————•◆•———————

Chapter 11: After-Death Communication

Three weeks after Sylvia's 42 year old partner died suddenly, a hurricane took the roof off their home and dumped much of the furniture and belongings onto the sand. Sylvia's family came to the coast to help her salvage anything they could but it was a very hard loss. Other people thought it was devastating but Sylvia knew devastation from her partner's death. She was asked if she would rebuild and told others that she would as that was her home.

After her family had salvaged everything possible, Sylvia went back to the house alone and began to wander through it. Sylvia says, "I stopped for a minute because I felt a hand on my leg just above my ankle. I looked down and heard very clearly my partner's voice saying, 'Sell it'. I realized that I was standing in the exact place where I had found her dead." Sylvia sold the property.

"Her presence was around me for many years and I have received much support and confirmation for my decisions. I occasionally still know she is there after 11 years. This experience confirmed for me that there is indeed "life after death." Now, I not only believe, I know."

Sylvia's uncle died suddenly after a brief illness. She went to spend the night with her aunt and was awakened in the middle of the night. She reported seeing her uncle (very transparent) sitting in the rocking chair across the room. She wondered how he was sitting there because she had thrown her suitcase in the same chair. Her uncle told her he had not been ready to die. He seemed bewildered and sat there for almost an hour. Sylvia told him to leave and that she would ask her parents, both deceased, to show him the way. He left and has not been heard from since.

While making the bed in her room, Sylvia noticed that the window suddenly closed by itself (no wind). "I knew it was Betty. She had been ill and was in the hospital. She had come to tell me good-bye." Within minutes, a mutual friend called and told her that Betty had passed away that morning.

Even though Sylvia was divorced after a 30 year marriage, her daughters asked her to help them when their father died. The funeral was planned and arrangements were made to have the service in his home state. During the funeral services, Sylvia reports that she saw him sitting in the front row, dressed in his suit with his arm on the back of the pew. He was looking at her and their daughters with a smile on his face.

"My daughter died suddenly at the age of 42 and we were all distraught. She and her husband had a 17 and a 6 year old. The week after the cremation, she woke me at 2:43 in the morning and said, 'Mom, I am all right. I love you, my nephew, my niece, my husband, my friend'... My mind questioned her appearance because she did not list the people she loved in the order that I thought she would. Suddenly, the voice of my mother said in a very matter of fact tone, 'She is with me and is all right.' My daughter came back two nights later to tell me that she was better, that it is so beautiful here.' I started talking to her in my head and she said, 'Mom, let me do the talking.' Sounded just like her, how comforting."

Linda's daughter, Lori, had a fascination with

Tinkerbell and even dressed up like her on her last Halloween. (Lori died three months later in an automobile accident.) Linda has pictures of her as Tinkerbell all over the house. Linda says," I can't tell you how many times while driving, I look at the car in front of me and it is covered with Tinkerbell decals. I never saw Tinkerbell on a car before Lori died. I know Tinkerbell sightings are just another way for Lori to get my attention to let me know she is with me.

Linda reported that the most "incredible" incident happened at the first Compassionate Friends Candle Lighting Ceremony she attended. She had gone with her other daughter, a friend and her own brother. She and her daughter stood together and unknown to her, photographers were taking pictures of the event. The next day Linda received a message from her friend telling her that a picture of her and her daughter were in the paper. Linda got the paper and said she was stunned. "I could not believe my eyes. Standing next to me was Lori not her sister. I kept looking at the picture thinking my eyes were playing tricks on me. The more I looked the more convinced that it was Lori. I remembered that during the ceremony I had asked for a sign from Lori that she was still with us. I definitely got my sign."

About six months after Lori's death, Linda was feeling desperate to know how she was. She scheduled an appointment with a psychic in an attempt to contact her. Linda stated that she spoke to Lori in her mind all the time. Prior to the reading, Linda had told Lori that she would know if the psychic had truly contacted her if she brought up Thanksgiving. Since her reading was in July, she felt this would be a true sign. During the reading Linda said she was told that Lori was trying to tell her something about Thanksgiving. Linda said, "You could have knocked me over with a feather! I had not told a soul about my secret code with Lori."

Two days after Jonathan was murdered, Pam was having a fitful night and kept going in and out of sleep. At one point, she woke up with a feeling that she was being touched. It was a hard slapping on the top of her hand. Pam said, "I woke up and no one was with me. I ran out of the room. My hand was red. I was frightened, uneasy and unable to understand what was happening to me. I felt that in my grief, I had truly lost my mind. I felt that it must have been Jonathan because when he was small he would come in my room at night and pat my hand to wake me up. I just did not know at the time that these types of things happened."

———◆◆◆———

Some who read these accounts may be distressed because they have never had an ADC. They may question themselves or their relationship with the deceased and wonder why it has not happened to them. Unfortunately, it is not really known why some people receive these contacts and others do not. There is no known correlation between being contacted and the nature of the relationship. Not having an ADC does not indicate that the loving bond that was there has been diminished. The belief is that anyone has the potential for having these experiences, but not everyone is aware and receives them. Often intense grief, fear and anger can serve as a block to awareness. Prayer and meditation are often suggested as ways to help facilitate communication.

Chapter 12: History and Theory

"You don't change the course of history by turning the faces of portraits to the wall."
Jawaharal Nehru

While the fascination with deathbed visions has ancient roots, the more contemporary work was begun in the early twentieth century. Psychical researchers such as F.W.H. Myers and James Hyslop both published accounts of deathbed visions in 1903 and 1907 respectively. In 1926, Sir William Barrett published *Deathbed Visions*[1] which was the first systematic study of the phenomenon. Barrett stated "There are a great many records authenticated by those who have attended the last moments of a dying friend or patient, wherein shortly before death an ecstatic vision seems to have been granted to the dying person, whose face lights up with joy and apparent recognition of some relative before he passes into the Unseen." While these words describe experiences of people in the early 1900's, they are just as descriptive of deathbed visions today. Barrett goes on to say, "Such cases are not confined to one country or one nation, but they appear to be more or less common all over the world."

In 1977, Dr.Karlis Osis along with Dr. Erlendur Haraldsson published *At the Hour of Death*,[2] a culmination of their research on cross cultural deathbed visions. This research was one of the earliest attempts to scientifically investigate life after death. Theirs was a four year study involving one thousand physicians and nurses in the United States and India. The focus of the work was not on the impact these experiences had on medical personnel, but rather the impact on patients. Nevertheless, some physicians and nurses noted that, by being witness to these events, their perspective on life and death changed. The results of the study were intriguing. In both cultures, deathbed visions were found to occur relatively independent of age, sex, ethnicity, education, religion, socioeconomic class, illness, or medical conditions (e.g. high fever). The typical vision was of a deceased family member coming to take away the dying patient. While the structural elements of DBVs were the same in America and India, there were some differences noted. The Indian population saw more religious figures and males than the American sample. As noted in Chapter 8, the Indian population also experienced more negative emotions such as fear and anxiety related to their deathbed vision. Nevertheless, the majority of both populations found comfort in the positive visions. A specific focus of Osis and Haraldsson's work was to investigate postmortem survival (life after death) based on deathbed visions. The authors concluded that their evidence was strongly suggestive of life after death. While not the focus of this book, a precursory examination of the debate on postmortem survival seems indicated to help the reader become more familiar with the controversy surrounding these experiences. Whether it is called "Survival vs. Destruction Doctrine"[2] the "Afterlife Hypothesis vs. the Dying Brain Hypothesis"[3]; or "Personal Continuance View vs. Finalistic View"[4], the issue is do we survive death?

One school of thought is that death is final and that we cease to exist in any form. In this view, deathbed visions are simply reflective of the dying process and represent hallucinatory phenomenon. Hallucinations are internally generated perceptions that occur when awake as opposed to visions or dreams that occur while one is asleep. They have little, if any, basis in reality and may involve any sensory modality (e.g. auditory, visual, olfactory, gustatory, and tactile). Auditory hallucinations are the most commonly occurring in certain types of psychosis, such as in schizophrenia.[5]

The second position is that the soul/spirit moves on after death to another plane of existence, usually to be reunited with loved ones. Hallucinations are used by both schools of thought to prove their respective positions. Researchers have reported that deathbed "hallucinations" differ from traditional hallucinations in that they tend to have a visual component. The dying are most likely to see deceased relatives or other spiritual beings with the intent of taking them away to another existence. Hence, these visions generally tend to have a calming effect on the patient. By contrast, traditional hallucinations tend to be viewed as "alien", threatening, or at least disquieting. Finally, in deathbed visions, otherworldly figures are usually seen, while with traditional hallucinations, figures more often take the form of images or individuals existing in the here and now.

In addition to trying to understand the meaning of these phenomena, there are also theories that attempt to help explain how these events happen in the first place. Herein lies even more controversy. There are four primary views that are proposed as explanations for these visions and experiences. The first is the dying brain theory proposed by Susan Blackmore in *Dying to Live*.[3] Dr. Blackmore, a psychologist and researcher, essentially states that as the brain dies there is a lack of oxygen and an increase in carbon dioxide which account for the visions. The combination of stress, fear and lack of oxygen can produce uncontrolled activity in the brain creating these experiences. At the time of death, there is also a release of endorphins or opiates that produce euphoria. (While this might serve to explain pleasant experiences, it certainly would not apply to the distressing ones.) The role of medications, brain chemicals and receptor sites have also been hypothesized to affect what one sees on dying. Essentially, these theories say that in the dying brain, visions and experiences are an artifact of brain chemistry.

The second theory centers on the role of temporal lobe epilepsy as the source of hallucinations or visions at death. With temporal lobe seizures, the individual can experience complex hallucinations that can involve both sounds and visual images. Britton and Boozin[6] found altered temporal lobe functioning in those who experienced NDEs. They found psychophysiological differences in this group as compared to a group of trauma survivors. Indeed, many researchers now believe that distressing experiences are mediated through the left temporal lobe and pleasant experiences through the right temporal lobe.

The most recent body based theory is that of REM, rapid eye movement, intrusions. In REM intrusion, some of the characteristics of sleep such as dreaming, atonia or paralysis occur (become active) during the transition from sleep to wakefulness. REM intrusion is a common feature of narcolepsy, a neurological disorder characterized by hallucinations, out-of-body experiences (OBEs) and episodes of uncontrollable sleep. In 2006, Nelson, Mattingly, Lee and Schmitt[7] compared people who had experienced NDEs and those who had not. They found that those who had experienced an NDE were more likely (60%) to experience problems in their sleep/wake cycle. It is not clear however if the NDE or the sleep disturbance came first. A REM intrusion tends to be a frightening experience while the majority of NDEs are viewed as calming and peaceful. Research in this area is ongoing.

The next theory centers on psychological factors that may explain the images seen by the dying. This position states that our fear of death is what creates what we see. It is a form of wish fulfillment where we see what we want to see as a way of comforting ourselves on dying. The pleasant visions as well as denial are in the service of the ego and are a psychological defense to dying.

The last theory is quite simple. It states that these visions are spiritual experiences that prove that there is a soul and a life after death. Patrick Glynn in his book *God: the Evidence*[8] indeed states that NDEs provide the first compelling scientific evidence for the independent existence of the soul. This spiritual theory has become the most controversial issue of all and has generated extensive exploration on both sides of the argument.

Man has been searching for the site in our bodies in which the soul resides since the time of Descartes. A philosopher, in the fifteenth century, Descartes believed that the pineal gland was the seat of the soul. Melvin Morse[9] asserts that the temporal lobe actually may be a mediating bridge for spiritual experiences. He refers to it as the "God Spot" or "the place where God lives in us all." Gregg Braden, [10] author of *The God Code* states that God lives in our DNA. Saver and Rabin[11], writing about the neural substrates or neurological mechanisms of religious experience, address all the brain/body based theories by stating that "determining the neural substrates of these states does not automatically lessen or demean their spiritual significance." Dr. Sam Parnia,[12] another cardiologist who has studied NDEs occurring during cardiac arrest, also acknowledges that while the exact areas of the brain that create these types of experiences are still unknown, it is clear that brain functioning mediates them. It seems then that it is possible to embrace a combination of the physical and spiritual explanation for these phenomena, since it appears that neither position offers a definitive explanation of the entire process.

Chapter 13: Nursing, Individuals and Spirituality

"The purpose of life is to live a life of purpose."
Robert Byrne

Prior to her seventeenth birthday, Florence Nightingale is said to have received a calling from God to nurse the sick. Nightingale held strong spiritual beliefs which formed the basis for all her work and her theory of nursing. Her philosophy was a holistic one, in which nursing care was to include both the body and spirit of the patient. Said to be a pragmatist, Nightingale also wanted nursing to maintain legitimacy and viability as a profession. In order to achieve this, she encouraged a focus on allopathic (conventional) medicine as well as spiritual care.

Over the years, some believe that modern nursing has lost its balance between body and spirit, with many nurses choosing to focus on the purely medical aspects of care.[1] Both nurses and doctors tend to see death as a failure and a negative reflection of their skills. Thus the focus in our culture has been almost exclusively on maintaining or restoring physical health rather than holistic, compassionate care.

Recently, Florence Nightingale's spiritual legacy has received renewed attention through the Holistic Nursing movement. Bradshaw[2] advocates that nurses should return to the vision of Nightingale in which they also address the spiritual needs of the patients and their families. Some even express the belief that spiritual nursing care is a professional, ethical and legal obligation.[3] Highfield, Taylor and Amenta[4] found that providing spiritual care to the dying enhances the personal spirituality of nurses. Spirituality is defined as a personal relationship with God, as opposed to religion which is a group's perception of God. Of course, these need not be mutually exclusive. One can be religious and spiritual at the same time. However to be spiritual suggests that through one's personal relationship with God, a broader, more universal view of life and God are developed. A nurse does not need to have religious training in order to provide spiritual care. Miller-Brown's[5] findings suggest that spirituality is not something that is learned from a book or a pulpit but rather is the result of an individual's choice to be compassionate and caring. In the current survey, virtually all the nurses reported viewing themselves as spiritual, including the nurses who had never experienced a DBV. Even though nurses may view themselves as spiritual, they are not always able to translate their spirituality into their care for the dying. Costello[6] found while nurses reported that addressing the spiritual and emotional needs of the dying was important, there was little evidence they did this in their practice. Other findings from Miller-Brown's research suggest that spirituality is necessary in nursing in order to find peace and meaning in their end-of-life work. She suggests that nurses who are comfortable with their own personal spirituality and who can find renewal through such things as prayer and meditation are the ones who cope the best with death in the work place

Dunn[7] found nurses believe that providing quality end of life care is important, independent of their feelings about death. There are, however, many obstacles that affect the nurses' ability to provide this care, including being overworked, poor communication among staff members about dying patients, disagreements with the physician's plan of care, burnout, lack of knowledge on how to talk with the dying, as well as the nurse's own attitude toward death. Rooda,[8] found the care that nurses provide to the dying patient may be affected by their own attitudes toward death, with those who have more experience with the dying having a more positive attitude. Nurses with a greater fear of death and reticence to talk about death had less positive attitudes toward caring for the dying.

When nurses are able to clarify their own views of death and the afterlife, it is easier to help others prepare for death as well as accepting one's own death and mortality. One nurse volunteered the following:

> *My first experience changed my whole perception of death and dying. It changed the way I care for patients and family members. It comforted the family when they learned that a relative or a friend was there to help their loved one make their final journey. I had one young man tell me that his biggest fear was dying alone. I assured him that he would not be alone when he started dying that someone would be there to help him transition from one life to the next. I have been a hospice nurse for four years, helping patients and families cope with the most trying times of their lives.*

Obviously not all patients or nurses feel comfortable discussing end of life issues and spirituality. While this must be respected, reports have appeared in the literature about the transformative power of deathbed experiences personally and professionally for nurses.[9,10] For some, simply hearing about deathbed visions can be spiritually transforming. The transformation often is a type of conversion experience that changes one's belief system and leads one to view life and death in a more positive way. In a description of her own NDE, Cheryl Powell, R.N.[11] states that after years of working in the ER and medical/surgical units she had lost faith in God. After her near-death experience, she commented that, "The reconnection with my spiritual side was not the only thing I gained from the experience. I also realized how important it is for nurses to be there, by the patient's side when death is near." Being physically present with a patient at the time of death is a theme often repeated by nurses in end-of-life care. A 2006 survey of members of the American Association of Critical Care Nurses found that the nurses placed great importance on patients' dying with dignity and on not dying alone.[12]

Chapter 14: Caring for the Caretaker

"The capacity to care is what gives life its deepest significance"
Pablo Casals

As death approaches, nurses are there to comfort the patient and family in their grief, but nurses can experience their own grief when a patient dies. The medical culture, however, makes grieving at work an unacceptable option. Unfortunately, grieving alone or disenfranchised grief is a part of nursing. Chronic compound grief occurs when staff is unable to process the loss of one patient before another dies. Nurses should be encouraged to recognize and express their feelings about these events. Not doing so could lead to more prolonged psychological distress. Caretakers in trouble can exhibit a range of behaviors from becoming numb and insensitive to the needs of others, to exhibiting excessive personal involvement, secretiveness, over identification with the patient and withdrawal from interactions with other staff. Talking about and processing one's feelings often results in reducing this type of stress and helps prevent burnout.

It is often hard to find a balance between being emotionally available to patients and protecting oneself. This balance is much easier to obtain and maintain when an interdisciplinary approach is taken to the needs of the staff and the dying. Nurses, doctors, psychologists, clergy and social workers can form a bond of support for each other, noticing and assisting when one of the team is having trouble keeping such a balance. Working collaboratively can be of great benefit to the patient as well as to the caregivers. Extending this collaborative model to other medical settings would obviously be advantageous to all involved. However, instituting such a model in other hospital settings is likely to be a challenge since, with the exception of hospice nurses, working with the dying is generally not given a high priority. Many feel that when death is certain, the physical requirements of the patient are all that need to be addressed. Emotional and spiritual care is often abandoned at this time. Implementing this team approach would require a major attitudinal shift among hospital administrators and medical staff. People must begin to see death as an important stage of life and not something to be kept in the shadows. Perhaps having more knowledge about the different deathbed experiences will help promote this paradigm shift.

The emotional demands on caretakers can be overwhelming at times. When working with nurses, one cannot help notice that many appear to have lost the ability to adequately attend to their own emotional needs. Everyone and everything else comes first, leaving little left for themselves. Consequently their physical, emotional and sometimes even their spiritual health, as well as their relationships are put in jeopardy. Given the high levels of stress to which nurses are exposed, especially in critical care settings, it is important to maintain that balance between their personal and professional identities. They need to learn to be care-receivers, not just caregivers.

SELF CARE

There are certain basics that we all need for our well being. In working with the ill and dying, training should also focus on finding ways of reducing caregivers' stress. This might include both general strategies and specific techniques as listed below. While many of these may be familiar, they do bear repeating.

a. Get adequate sleep
b. Eat healthier foods
c. Exercise
d. Meet with friends on a regular basis
e. Have friends who are not in your profession, so you can focus on something besides work
f. While at times it seems like an impossibility, try to get some alone time at home where no one is asking anything of you
g. Sit and relax
h. Learn how to say no
i. Do not take on others' problems and try to fix them.

In addition to these basics, it is important to have multiple ways of coping when confronted with job related stress. There are a variety of techniques and procedures that can be helpful. Those presented here can be done in approximately five minutes. Many relaxation and calming procedures involve controlled breathing. A few examples are:

1) Sit comfortably, breathe naturally, and close your eyes. Every time a thought appears, place it in a balloon or bubble and let it fly away and disappear. You can do this until the thoughts are completely gone but five minutes should be sufficient.

2) The simplest form of meditation also involves focusing on breathing. Close your eyes. Sit comfortably and breathe in through your nose. While doing this, think to yourself, "I am breathing in and on the exhale through your mouth, I am breathing out." Do this until you feel more centered and calm.

3) A second breathing procedure involves inhaling

slowly to the count of four. Hold the breath to the count of four and then exhale to the count of four. The relaxation response is created by exaggerating the breath while inflating your lungs to the fullest and then exaggerating the breath when exhaling as though you were completely emptying your lungs.

4) Another technique that has been frequently used in therapy is creating a safe place. When you have time, think about a place where you have been or would like to go where you feel safe and secure. It can be a real or an imaginary place. What is there about this place that is so peaceful and secure for you? Think about the sights, sounds or smells of this special place. If you spend some time developing this place in your mind, it will be easier to call up if you find yourself in a stressful situation so you can take yourself there and begin to feel more at ease.

5) It is also important to think about what soothing procedures have worked the best for you in the past. Unfortunately many people soothe themselves by drinking, smoking or eating too much. Healthier choices may involve listening to music, exercising, sitting in a rocking chair, journaling, talking on the phone to a friend, doing Yoga, getting a massage, taking a hot bath or shower, having Healing Touch or Reiki sessions, or using aroma therapy.

Other soothing exercises come from the field of Energy Psychology. It is the branch of psychology that studies the effects of energy systems on emotions and behavior. Psychological as well as medical problems are said to reflect manifestations of energy disruption in which procedures such as acupressure and acupuncture are used.

For those interested in a more academic understanding of the field, Gallo[1] is recommended. There also are a number of books available for self healing that require no theoretical understanding but show specific procedures to use to address a wide range of psychological disturbances. [2,3]

One of the procedures is called Balanced Breathing. This involves sitting down, placing your right ankle over your left ankle, extending your arms and placing your right wrist over your left wrist. Placing your palms together, clasp your fingers and fold your hands and arms to rest on your chest. Once in that position, begin by taking deep cleansing breaths and then just breathe slowly and gently. Do this until you are comfortable with your breathing. Then, while focusing on your breathing, think about the word "balance." Next, visualize something that represents balance to you. It can be anything such as a scale or a see-saw. Stay like this until you feel more centered and connected. Most people only need two minutes to complete this. If you need longer, that's okay.

There are also several variations of eye-roll techniques that can be done in a short time period. Close your eyes. With your eyelids shut, roll your eyes upward as though you are trying to look at the top of your head. Keep your eyelids shut and roll your eyes down.[4] The other is a floor to ceiling eye-roll. Hold your head level and let your eyes focus on a corner of the room. Follow the line of the wall's intersection with your eyes only until your eyes are over your head.

Another self soothing technique is called the Chest Spot. The "spot" is located above the heart about three inches off the center line toward your left. This is often called the "sore spot" since it is frequently sore to the touch. Using your right hand, rub in a tight circular motion (at least three times) while saying, "Even though I have this (insert emotion here), I deeply and completely accept myself."

This procedure allows you to fill in any emotion you may be experiencing such as sadness or anxiety, telling yourself, "Even though I have this saddness, I deeply and completely accept myself."

The "Butterfly Hug" has been used successfully to treat traumatized children in Mexico.[5] It can also be helpful for adults.[6] Cross your arms over your chest. Place your right arm on your left shoulder and your left hand on your right shoulder. Alternately pat each shoulder. If this position is not comfortable use the same procedure but place your hands under the clavicle and pat. Find the position that is the most comfortable for you. While you are patting yourself, say a positive affirmation such as, "I can handle this" or "I can let this go."

An additional rapid stress reduction exercise is a variation of the Spiral Technique.[7] Close your eyes and focus on the emotion that you are feeling. Imagine it as energy moving. Notice in which direction it is moving, i.e. clockwise, counterclockwise. Now with your mind, move the energy in the opposite direction until you feel an internal shift. You could also picture the feeling as having a shape and color and changing it into a different color or shape that is more soothing or comfortable.

Finally, performing rituals is another way to soothe ourselves. Many religions use candles for prayers and mourning. Perhaps lighting an electric candle on the unit when a patient dies would be a small ritual that could be accompanied by a prayer. Other rituals could be developed by the staff on the unit that would be meaningful for all.

Chapter 15: Direction for the Caretaker

"Education is the movement from darkness to light."
Allan Bloom

As important as end of life care is, it is surprising how little academic education nurses receive in this area. A study in London found that patients would rather talk to nurses than physicians about their death bed experiences.[1] Without adequate preparation and training, how can nurses be expected to handle this most critical task at the end of life? Education on end-of-life issues continues to be limited in nursing curriculum, even though there has been a call for this for years. In fact, a 2006 survey of nurses examining how to improve end of life care revealed that nurses thought that their nursing education had not adequately prepared them to provide this crucial aspect of nursing and that they had "to learn the hard way."[2] In a 2003 survey by the now defunct Last Acts Campaign, a large coalition working for the improvement of end-of-life care, respondents rated every state in the United States as being mediocre or worse in the care of the dying. These results suggest a need to improve the education of nurses about death and dying and to offer specific training on end-of-life issues, both spiritual and medical, as separate subjects in their curriculum.[3]

Such a curriculum should include learning about all the various death related experiences as well as exploring their own attitudes toward death and developing ways of communicating with the dying. In addition to lectures, using films about the dying process, such as the documentary <u>Dying at Grace,</u>[4] allows people to connect with the subject matter on a more emotional rather than intellectual level. Other personal involvement could come through practicing skills through role playing.

SELF AWARENESS

In preparation for working with the dying, it is important for nurses to recognize their own attitudes, feelings, values and expectations regarding death, as well as having an opportunity to discuss their beliefs regarding death, the afterlife and bereavement. At some point in their careers most nurses are confronted with death. Having courses that specifically allow nurses an opportunity to explore their spirituality and delve more deeply into issues surrounding death would better prepare them to assist the patients and to understand and cope with their own feelings when faced with these situations. Coursework should provide not only didactic material about dying but also provide an opportunity for clarification of beliefs and values. However, it is never too late to do this self-exploration. Among the questions that all who work with the dying should be able to answer for themselves are:

What are my personal experiences with death?

How have I coped with loss in the past?

What do I fear the most about dying?

What do I think happens after death?

Has anyone in my family had an unusual death related experience?

What are my personal concerns about working with the dying?

What would be the worst thing that could happen to me while I lay dying?

The following questions allow you to contemplate your ideal death. This is another way to assess personal concerns, expectations, priorities and needs relating to death.

1) Where would you like to be when you die?
2) Who and what is around you?
3) What are you doing?
4) What are the people doing who are around you?
5) What has been happening in the last couple of days?
6) What has been happening in the last couple of hours?
7) What is the very last thing you do?
8) What is the very last thing you say?

Now that you have completed your ideal death, think about what you would *not* want to happen to you on your deathbed. Remember this when you work with the dying.

INTERACTING WITH THE DYING

Authors, Callanan and Kelly[5]; Hayes,[6] Wooten-Green[7] and Wills-Brandon,[8] agree that, listening to the patients, being supportive, as well as accepting of them and their accounts are all important skills in working with the dying, whether they are experiencing a DBV or NDE. It should be noted that the nurses in this survey appeared to be attentive, reassuring and were not dismissive of what the dying experienced. Learning to work with dying patients and their families involves knowing both what to do as well as what not to do. The American Academy of Bereavement (AAB) provides the following guidelines. First they list the "Do Nots", that is behaviors that will discourage interactions between the nurse and the patients and/or their families. They are:

1) Be Busy
2) Do not smile
3) Adapt a cold demeanor
4) Use an abrasive, harsh tone
5) Only use professional jargon
6) Ignore questions
7) Deflect requests for information
8) Ask closed questions
9) Do not make eye contact
10) Be mean. Argue with the patient
11) Try to force someone to accept his or her death
12) Try to convert someone on their deathbed
13) Talk about yourself
14) Negate their experiences

While such behaviors might initially be viewed as self-protective for the staff, obviously they are not in the best interest of the patients or their families. Ultimately, they are not in the best interest of the nurses either as they insulate them from the rewards of providing the support needed by those under their care.

There are behaviors designed to facilitate communication and support while potentially providing a greater sense of professional rewards for the nurses themselves. They are:

1) Let the dying take the lead. If they do not want to talk, do not force them.
2) Be respectful. Treat the dying with dignity.
3) Be present in the moment with the patient.
4) Be ready to listen. Listen from your heart.
5) Give time to the patient and family.
6) Be yourself.
7) Be non-judgmental.
8) Be sensitive.
9) Allow the dying to reminisce.
10) Be kind and considerate.

11) Let the dying talk about their feelings.
12) Laugh with them when they make jokes.
13) Realize you are human and that you can cry with them too.
14) Notice any nonverbal behaviors such as stares and smiles.
15) If you do not know what to say, do not say anything at all. You can smile at the patients or pat their hands.
16) Share the information with other caregivers.
17) Remember, hearing is the last sense to go. Be cautious of what you say around the dying.
18) Be compassionate.
19) Listen for their symbolic language
20) Treat them as you would want to be treated

Helping to alleviate the dying patient's physical pain is an important nursing function, but listening to their patients as they prepare to leave this world may be of even greater service to them. It is not necessary for the nurse to have a belief that what the patient is experiencing is real or not. It is not about the listener. It is about the patients and what can be provided for them. Simpson[9] advocates that given the number of individuals who have near death experiences, nurses should learn more about these phenomena. One could extrapolate from this that nurses should be encouraged to become familiar with all death related experiences. A study conducted in Australia[10] found that nurses felt the communication of paranormal experiences was important. However, ways of communicating and documenting the information were not consistent. While some nurses might be uncomfortable putting this information in the chart, having a book on the unit that would only be used to note paranormal experiences might be an alternative. Sharing these experiences in shift change could also serve to remind people of the true spiritual nature of their work as they begin their day.

Finally, David Kessler[11] has compiled a list of the needs of the dying of which all involved in their care should be familiar. They are:

1) "The need to be treated as a living human being.
2) The need to maintain a sense of hopefulness, however changing its focus may be.
3) The need to be cared for by those who can maintain a sense of hopefulness however changing this may be.
4) The need to express feelings and emotions about death in one's own way.
5) The need to participate in decisions concerning one's care.
6) The need to be cared for by compassionate, sensitive, knowledgeable people.
7) The need for continuing medical care, even though the goals may change from 'cure' to 'comfort' goals.
8) The need to have all questions answered honestly and fully.
9) The need to seek spirituality.
10) The need to be free of physical pain.
11) The need to express feelings and emotions about pain in one's own way.
12) The need for children to participate in death.
13) The need to understand the process of death.
14) The need to die in peace and dignity.
15) The need not to die alone.
16) The need to know that the sanctity of the body will be respected after death."

Chapter 16: Concluding Thoughts

"Death is only an experience through which you are meant to learn a lesson: you cannot die."
Paramahansa Yogananda

For many in the 21st century, death remains a taboo subject. So much fear and pain surrounds death that it is easier for most people to use denial as a way of not addressing the inevitable. Margaret Mead, the anthropologist, said, "When a person is born, we rejoice, and when they are married, we jubilate; but when they die, we try to pretend that nothing has happened." While we may fear death, for many the ultimate fear is that of dying alone. The volumes written over the years and the research done have not yet produced a paradigm shift in the way we think about death. People do not like to talk or think about death and therefore do not access the information that is available that could make their dying more peaceful. An example of this came from a hospice nurse I knew who told me about a man who thought that her job was to kill him with a lethal injection! One can only imagine his level of distress when he knew she was coming.

"There are two ways to live your life. One is as though nothing is a miracle; the other is as though everything is a miracle."
Albert Einstein, scientist

Birth and death are often spoken of as similar in that

each is an ushering into a new existence. There is a type of miracle surrounding each. However, while our joy allows us to see the one, our fear and pain often obliterates the other. There are special nurses for birthing called midwives or doulas. A birth doula is described as someone who "while helping with the birth process also engages parents to be in a transformational experience, a key life event full of emotion and meaning. A doula accompanies the woman in labor; mothers the mother and takes care of her emotional needs throughout the birthing process. A doula also provides support and suggestions for families that can enhance their experience. A post partum doula continues that valuable emotional support and guidance, helping a family make a smooth transition into new family dynamics."[1]

It is easy to see how by changing some of the above words, one could easily be describing perhaps a new specialty in nursing called a doula for the dying. For example, a doula for the dying might be characterized as someone helping with the dying process by engaging families in a "transformational experience, a key life event full of emotion and meaning". The doula for the dying could accompany the dying in their passing, "mother the dying," and take care of their emotional needs throughout the dying process. Such an individual might also provide support and suggestions for the families. After death, the doula could continue to be a resource for emotional support and guidance for family members needing additional assistance in transitioning to a new life without their loved one.

In order to do this work, it would be essential for a nurse (or anyone) to have a good understanding and acceptance of his or her own beliefs and attitudes about death, religion, spirituality, whether or not their beliefs include the existence of an afterlife. Any nurses who currently work with the dying must also have an opportunity to do their own grief work if for no other reason than to protect their own psyches. One of the nurses in the survey wrote that when she is around someone who is dying it brings back the painful memories of her husband's death "as if it had just happened." She further stated that she did not think that she would "ever get over his death" and talk about it with her children. This is an example of how doing one's own grief work is essential. Imagine how much pain she must experience by constantly being confronted with death in her position in a nursing home.

As we die, there is something amazing happening. Those of us who are researchers get caught up in whether or not these DBV's are real or not and the source of their origin. In part, perhaps this is just another way in which we have to distance ourselves from what is happening. It appears that in the process of trying to understand death bed experiences we are missing the bigger picture. Do you think that as one lies dying that he or she really cares what causes these visions? It is doubtful. This is real for them. With the positive experiences, patients are no longer afraid and are at peace. This is a priceless gift no matter where it comes from and what triggers it. Both nurse and patient are able to share this "holy ground"[2] at the hour of death. This is a type of miracle whether or not it comes from God or that our brain chemistry allows us to die in this way. The fact that we could be comforted in such a way is amazing by itself. Picture yourself on your death bed and one of your deceased parents, children or spouse comes to reassure you that things will be fine and that they will take care of you. How much more comforting can that be as we face death? Perhaps instead of a family member, you see Christ, an angel or some other heavenly being. It is not known if these visions prove the existence of an afterlife but what a gift of comfort we receive as we leave this world. In our final moments, is that not what we all want?

Author's Notes

Chapter 1: Introduction
1. Callanan, Maggie and Kelley, Patricia. (1992). *Final Gifts: Understanding the Special Awareness, Needs, and Communications of the Dying*, New York: Bantam Books.
2. Morse, Melvin. (1994). *Parting Visions*, New York: Villard Books.
3. Kubler-Ross, Elizabeth. (1991). *On Life After Death*, Berkeley, California: Celestial Arts.
4. Ethier, Angela M. (2005). *"Death Related Sensory Experiences"*. Journal of Pediatric Oncology Nursing, 22 (2), 104-110.
5. January, 2007, retrieved from www. findadeath.com/ deceased/k/kinison/ samkinison.htm).
6. Zaleski, Carol. (1987). *Otherworld Journeys: Accounts of Near Death Experiences in Medieval and Modern Times*, New York: Oxford University Press.
7. Stanworth, Rachel. (2002). *"Attention: A potential vehicle for spiritual care"*. Journal of Palliative Care, 18: 3, 192-195.

Chapter 2: Accounts of Dead Relatives
1. Osis, Karlis and Haraldsson, Erlendur. (1997) *At the Hour of Death*, 2nd edition, Norwark, Connecticut: Hastings House.

Chapter 3: Jesus and Angels
1. Morse, Melvin. (1994). *Parting Visions*, New York: Villard Books.

Chapter 6: Silent Deathbed Visions
1. Blackmore, Susan. (1993). *Dying to Live: Science and the Near Death Experience*, London: Grafton.
2. Fox, Mark. (2003). *Religion, Spirituality and the Near Death Experience*. New York and London: Routledge.
3. Ring, Kenneth and Valarino, Evelyn. (2006). *Lessons From The Light*, 2nd edition, Needham, Massachusetts: Moment Point Press.
4. Irwin, H.J. (1987). *"Out of Body Experiences in the Blind"*. Journal of Near Death Studies, 6, 53-60.

Chapter 7: Other Types of Visions

1. Rainbows are the second most common form of after-death communication.
2. Osis, Karlis and Haraldsson, Erlendeur. (1997) *At the Hour of Death*, 2nd edition, Norwark, Connecticut: Hastings House.

Chapter 8: Distressing Deathbed Visions

1. Kubler-Ross, Elizabeth. (1969). *On Death and Dying*. New York: MacMillan.
2. Osis, Karlis and Haraldsson, Erlendeur. (1997) *At the Hour of Death*, 2nd edition, Norwark, Connecticut: Hastings House.
3. *Koran*. (2004). Translated by J.M. Rodwell. London: Phoenix.
4. Rinpoche, Sogyal. (1993). *The Tibetan Book of Living and Dying*, San Francisco: Harper.
5. Raphael, Simca Paull. (2004). *Jewish Views of the Afterlife*, Northvale, N.J.: Jason Aronson.
6. Blackmore, Susan. (1993) *Dying to Live: Science and the Near Death Experience*, London: Grafton.
7. Houran, James and Lange, Rense. (1997) *"Hallucinations that Comfort: Contextual Mediation of Deathbed Visions"*. Perceptual and Motor Skills, 84, 1491-1504.
8. Osis, Karlis and Haraldsson, Erlendur. (1997) *At the Hour of Death*, 2nd edition, Norwark, Connecticut: Hastings House.
9. Greyson, Bruce and Bush, Nancy Evans (1992) *"Distressing Near Death Experiences"*. Psychiatry, vol. 55, 95-110.
10. Evans-Wentz, W.Y. (2000). *The Tibetan Book of the Dead*. Oxford: University Press.
11. *Holy Bible: King James Version* (1979) Wheaton, Illinois, Tyndale House Publisher Inc.
12. Moody, Raymond. (2001) *Life After Life*, 2nd edition, San Francisco, California: Harper.
13. Atwater, P.M.H. and Morgan, David H. (2000). *The Complete Idiots Guide to Near Death Experiences*, Indianapolis, Indiana: Alpha Books.

14. Bush, N.E. (2000). *"Afterward: Making meaning after a frightening near-death experience"*. Journal of Near-Death Studies 21(2), 99-133.

15. Rommer, Barbara. (2000). *Blessing in disguise: Another side of the Near Death Experience*. St. Paul, MN: Llewellyn.

16. d'Aquili, Eugene and Newberg, Andrew B. (1999). *The Mystical Mind: Probing the Biology of Religious Experience*. Minneapolis: Fortress Press.

17. Zaleski, Carol. (1987). *Otherworld Journeys: Accounts of Near Death Experiences in Medieval and Modern Times*, New York: Oxford University Press.

18. Rawlings, Maurice. (1993). *To Hell and Back*, Nashville Thomas Nelson Publishers.

19. Dr. Rawlings chastises those who have not talked about these Hellish experiences in their research. He proclaims that the only way to avoid these distressing experiences is to be a Christian. While his findings about the occurrence of frightening experiences have not been in question, his interpretations based on his fundamentalist Christian views are offensive to many. His position however does not explain how people from non-Christian cultures have positive experiences and visions of Heaven.

20. Storm, Howard. (2005). *My Descent into Death: Second chance at life*, New York: Doubleday.

Chapter 9: Near Death Experiences

1. Eadie, Betty J. (1992). *Embraced by the Light*. Placerville, California: Putman Press.

2. Moody, Raymond. (2001) *Life After Life*, 2nd edition, San Francisco, California: Harper.

3. Bailey, Lee W. and Yates, Jenny (eds) (1996). *The Near Death Experience: A Reader*, New York and London: Routledge.

4. Zhi-ying, Feng and Jian-xun, Liu. (1992). *"Near Death Experiences among Survivors of the 1976 Tangshan Earthquake"*. Journal of Near-Death Studies, 11(1) Fall, 39-48.

Chapter 10: Dreams

1. Bulkeley, Kelly and Bulkley, Patricia. (2005). *Dreaming Beyond Death: A Guide to Pre-Death Dreams and Visions*, Boston: Beacon Press.

2. Cartwright, Rosalind and Lamberg, Lynne. (1992). *Crisis Dreaming, Using Your Dreams to Solve Your Problems*, New York: Harper Perennial.

3. Garfield, Patricia (1996). *"Dreams in Bereavement"*. Deidre Barnett (Ed.) Trauma and Dreams (pp186-211), Cambridge Massachusetts: Harvard University Press.

4. Guggenheim, Bill and Guggenheim, Judy. (1996). *Hello From Heaven*. New York: Bantam Books.

5. Wray, T.J. (2005) *Grief Dreams*, San Francisco California: Jossey-Bass.

6. Those who are familiar with the Bible may find it interesting to note that her comment is reminiscent of that found in John 21:17 in the New Testament in which Jesus says to Mary Magdalene. "Touch me not for I have not yet ascended to my Father."

Chapter 11: After Death Communications

1. Guggenheim, Bill and Guggenheim, Judy. (1996). *Hello From Heaven*. New York: Bantam Books.

2. This account is a good example of synchronicity. A synchronicity is a meaningful coincidence. Such coincidences occur frequently in our daily lives. Almost everyone has had an experience of thinking of someone and then unexpectedly seeing them or receiving a phone call. It is the timing of these experiences in after death communications that make them so convincing and compelling as in this account.

Chapter 12: History and Theory

1. Barrett, Sir William.(1986). *Death-Bed Visions: The Psychical Experiences of the Dying*. London: Psychic Press, 1926 Reprint. Northamptonshire, England: The Aquarian Press.

2. Osis, Karlis and Haraldsson, Erlendur. (1997) *At the Hour of Death*, 2nd edition, Norwark, Connecticut: Hastings House.

3. Blackmore, Susan. (1993). *Dying to Live: Science and the Near Death Experience*, London: Grafton.
4. Berger, Arthur and Berger, Joyce. (1995). *Fear of the Unknown Enlightened Aid in Dying*. Westport, CT: Praeger Publishers.
5. Visual, tactual, olfactory and even gustatory hallucinations are known to accompany various other medical conditions.
6. Britton, Willoughby and Bootzin, Richard. (2004). *"Near-Death Experiences and the Temporal Lobe"*. Psychological Science, 15 (4),254-258.
7. Nelson, Kevin R., Mattingly, Michelle, Lee, Sherman A. and Schmitt, Frederick A. (2006) *"Does the arousal system contribute to near death experience?"* Neurology, 66, 1003-1009.
8. Glynn, Patrick (1997) *God the Evidence: The Reconciliation of Faith and Reason in a Post Secular World*. Prima Publishing, Rocklin: California.
9. Morse, Melvin. (2000) *Where God Lives*, New York: Harper Collins.
10. Braden, Greg. (2004). *The God Code: The Secret of our Past, the Promise of our Future*, Carlsbad, California: Hay House.
11. Saver, Jeffrey L. and Rabin, John. (1997). *"The Neural Substrates of Religious Experience"*. In Salloway, Stephen, Mallory, Paul and Cummings, Jeffrey (Ed.) The Neuropsychiatry of Limbic and Subcortical Disorders (pp 195-207), Washington, D.C.: American Psychiatric Press, Inc.
12. Parnia, Sam. (2006). *What Happens When We Die*, Carlsbad, California: Hay House.

Chapter 13: Nursing, Individuals and Spirituality
1. Light, Kathleen. (1997, March). *"Florence Nightingale and the Wholistic Philosophy"*. Journal of Holistic Nursing, 15(1), 25-40.
2. Bradshaw, Ann. (1996). *"The Legacy of Nightingale"*. Nursing Times, 92(6), 42-43.
3. Wright, K.B. (1998). *"Professional, Ethical and Legal*

Implications for Spiritual Care in Nursing". Journal of Nursing Scholarship, 30, 81-83.

4.   Highfield, M.E., Taylor, E.J., and Amenta, M.O. (2000). *"Preparation to Care: The spiritual care education on oncology patients and hospice nurses"*. Journal of Hospice and Palliative Nursing, 2(2), 53-63.

5.   Miller-Brown, K.E. (2000). *"Nurses' Experiences with Spirituality and End of Life Care"*. Unpublished doctoral dissertation, University Alabama at Birmingham, Alabama.

6.   Costello, John. (2001). *"Nursing Older Dying Patients: Findings from an ethnographic study of death and dying in elderly care wards"*. Journal of Advanced Nursing, 35(1), 59-68.

7.   Dunn, Karen S., Otten, Cecelia, and Stephens, Elizabeth. (2005). *"Nursing Experience and the Care of Dying Patients"*. Oncology Nursing Forum, Vol.32 No.1, 97-103.

8.   Rooda, Linda, Clements, Richard and Jordan, Marcia. (1999). *"Nurses Attitudes toward Death and Caring for Dying Patients"*, Oncology Nursing Forum, Vol 26, No. 10, 1683-1687.

9.   Davis, Mary G. (1998). *"I Need to Tell Someone about what I saw."* Nursing, December-32cc, 6-8.

10. Ethier, Angela, M. (2005). *"Death-Related Sensory Experiences"*. Journal of Pediatric Oncology Nursing, 22 (2), 104-110.

11. Powell, Cheryl. (1999). *"Near Death: A Nurse Reflects"*. RN 62(4), 43-44

12. Beckstrand, Renea, Callister, Lynn Clark and Kirchhoff, Karin (2006). *"Providing a 'Good Death': Critical Care Nurses' Suggestions for Improving End of Life Care"*. American Journal of Critical Care, 15, 38-45.

Chapter 14: Caring For The Caretaker

1.   Gallo, Fred. (1999). *Energy Psychology: Explorations at the interface of Energy, Cognition, Behavior, and Health.* Boca Ratan, Florida: CRC Press LLC.

2.   Eden, Donna. (1998). *Energy Medicine: Balance Your*

Body's Energies for Optimum Health, Joy, and Vitality.
New York: Jeremy P. Tarcher/Putman.

3. Lambrou, Peter and Pratt, George. (2000). *Acupressure for the Emotions.* New York: Broadway Books.

4. Temes, Roberta. (2000) *The Complete Idiot's Guide to Hypnosis.* Indianapolis, Indiana: Alpha Books.

5. Tinker R.H. and Wilson, S.A. (1999). *Through the Eyes of a Child: EMDR with Children.* New York: Norton.

6. More information on tapping can be found in Laurel Parnell's 2008 book, *Tapping In: A Step-by-Step Guide to Activating Your Healing Resources Through Bilateral Stimulation.*

7. Shapiro, Francine. (2001) *Basic Principles, Protocols and Procedure,* second edition. New York, New York: The Guilford Press.

Chapter 15: Instruction for the Caretaker

1. Brayne, Sue, Farnham, Chris and Fenwick Peter. (2006) *"Deathbed phenomena and their effect on a palliative care team: a pilot study".* American Journal of Hospice and Palliative Care, Jan-Feb; 23(1): 17-24.

2. Beckstrand, Renea, Callister, Lynn Clark and Kirchhoff, Karin (2006). *"Providing a 'Good Death': Critical Care Nurses' Suggestions for Improving End of Life Care".* American Journal of Critical Care, 15, 38-45.

3. Thompson, Gelene. (2005). *"Effects of End of Life Education on Baccalaureate Nursing Students".* Association of PeriOperative Registered Nurses' Journal (AORN), 82:6, 434.

4. King, Allan (Director). *Dying At Grace*: 2003 documentary, Canada

5. Callanan, Maggie and Kelley, Patricia. (1992). *Final Gifts: Understanding the Special Awareness, Needs and Communications of the Dying,* New York: Bantam Books.

6. Hayes, Evelyn, Hardie, Thomas, Bucher, Linda, and Wimbush, Frances. (1998). *"Near Death: Back from Beyond",* RN 61(12), 54-58

7. Wooten-Green, Ron. (2001). *When the Dying Speak,* Chicago, Illinois: Loyola Press.

8. Wills-Brandon, Carla. (2005). *One Last Hug Before I Go: the mystery and meaning of deathbed visions*, Deerfield Beach, Florida: Health Communications, Inc.

9. Simpson, Suzanne. (2001). *"Near Death Experiences: a concept analysis as applied to nursing"*. Journal of Advanced Nursing, 36(4), 520-526.

10. O'Conner, Deborah (2003). *"Palliative Care Nurses' Experiences of Paranormal Phenomena and Their Influence on Nursing Practice"*. Paper Presented at the Making Sense of Dying and Death Interdisciplinary Conference, Paris, France.

11. Kessler, David. (2007). *The Needs of the Dying*, 10th anniversary edition. New York: HarperCollins.

Chapter 16: Concluding Thoughts

1. Doulas of North America @ www.dona.org.

2. O'Brien, Mary Elizabeth. (2003). *Spirituality in Nursing*, 2nd edition Sudbury, Massachusetts: Jones and Bartlett Publishers.

Appendix A
Summary of Nurses' Reponses to Questionnaire

1. RN <u>221</u>   LPN <u>13</u>

2. Specialty area: Home Health <u>7%</u> Hospice <u>16%</u> Nursing Home <u>2%</u> ICU <u>16%</u>   Med/Surg <u>21%</u> Oncology <u>14%</u> Skilled Care <u>5%</u> Other <u>19%</u>

3. How many years have you been a nurse? 0-5 <u>15%</u> 6-10 <u>19%</u> 11-15 <u>14%</u> 16-20 <u>13%</u> 20+ <u>39%</u>

4. Have you ever witnessed a patient having a deathbed vision?
    Yes <u>65%</u>   No <u>35%</u>

Please answer questions 5-13 only if you have ever witnessed a deathbed vision.

5. How many deathbed visions have you witnessed? 1-2 <u>43%</u> 3-4 <u>24%</u>   5-6 <u>11%</u> 7-8 <u>5%</u> 9+ <u>17%</u>

6. In most cases, did the patients' overall reactions to this experience seem mostly: Positive <u>86%</u> Negative 3% Neutral <u>11%</u>

7. What is the most common type of Deathbed Vision(s) you have witnessed? Visions of: Dead Relative <u>57%</u> Living relative <u>6%</u> Religious figure <u>13%</u> Beautiful Scenery <u>12%</u> Other <u>12%</u>

8. Do you consider yourself to be a fairly spiritual person? Yes <u>93%</u> No <u>5%</u> Uncertain <u>2%</u>

9. Did you interpret the patient's deathbed visions as most likely representing: A spiritual phenomenon <u>85%</u> A delirious/hallucinatory phenomenon <u>15%</u>

10. How would you classify your feelings about the patient's deathbed vision experience? Spiritually moving <u>36%</u> Comforting <u>51%</u> Confusing <u>3%</u> Uncomfortable <u>3%</u> Frightening <u>2%</u> Indifferent <u>4%</u> Other <u>1%</u>

11. Did you talk about this experience(s) with anyone? Yes <u>89%</u> No <u>11%</u>

The majority of nurses spoke with more than one person. The order of frequency with whom they spoke is given below with 1 being the most frequent and 4, the least frequent.

If yes, who was this person? Another Health Care Provider: _1_ Friend: _3_ Family: _2_ Clergy: _4_ Other: <u>family of patient</u>

If not, why not? Only one person responded to this question saying, <u>"I just don't like talking about death."</u>

12. In terms of your perception of the dying experience, did the deathbed vision(s) make you: More comfortable <u>76%</u> less comfortable <u>4%</u> or had no effect <u>20%</u>

13. Do you believe you are now more open to talking to your patients about dying as a result of having witnessed a deathbed vision? Yes <u>65%</u> No <u>7%</u> No Change <u>28%</u>

Other Publications from ICAN Publishing, Inc.

NURSING MADE INSANELY EASY!

PHARMACOLOGY MADE INSANELY EASY!

NCLEX-RN® 101: How To Pass!

PATHWAYS TO TEACHING NURSING: KEEPING IT REAL!

SEEKING SAFETY:
The Journey of Adults Who Were
Sexually Abused as Children

Contact us at
ICAN Publishing, Inc.
162 Lumpkin County Parkway
Dahlonega, Georgia 30533
1.866.428.5589
or online at
www.icanpublishing.com